LESSON PLAN BOOK

Great Source Education Group
a Houghton Mifflin Company
Wilmington, Massachusetts

www.greatsource.com

AUTHORS

Laura Robb
Author

Powhatan School, Boyce, Virginia
Laura Robb, author of *Reading Strategies That Work* and *Teaching Reading in Middle School*, has taught language arts at Powhatan School in Boyce, Virginia, for more than 30 years. She is a co-author of the *Reading and Writing Sourcebooks* for grades 3–5 and the *Summer Success: Reading* program. Robb also mentors and coaches teachers in Virginia public schools and speaks at conferences throughout the country on reading and writing.

Ron Klemp
Contributing Author

Los Angeles Unified School District, Los Angeles, California
Ron Klemp is the Coordinator of Reading for the Los Angeles Unified School District. He has taught Reading, English, and Social Studies and was a middle school Dean of Discipline. He is also coordinator/facilitator at the Secondary Practitioner Center, a professional development program in the Los Angeles Unified School District. He has been teaching at California State University, Cal Lutheran University, and National University.

Wendell Schwartz
Contributing Author

Adlai Stevenson High School, Lincolnshire, Illinois
Wendell Schwartz has been a teacher of English for 36 years. For the last 24 years he also has served as the Director of Communication Arts at Adlai Stevenson High School. He has taught gifted middle school students for the last 12 years, as well as teaching graduate-level courses for National-Louis University in Evanston, Illinois.

Editorial:
Design:
Illustrations:

Developed by Nieman, Inc.
Ronan Design: Christine Ronan, Sean O'Neill, and Maria Mariottini
Mike McConnell

Trademarks and trade names are shown in this book strictly for illustrative purposes and are the property of their respective owners. The author's references herein should not be regarded as affecting their validity.

Copyright © 2002 by Great Source Education Group, Inc. All rights reserved.
Great Source ® is a registered trademark of Houghton Mifflin Company.

Where specifically noted, as on pages 14–15, permission is hereby granted to teachers to reprint or photocopy pages in the *Lesson Plan Book* in classroom quantities for use in their classes with accompanying Great Source material. Such copies may not be sold, and further distribution is expressly prohibited. Except as authorized above, prior written permission must be obtained from Great Source Education Group, Inc., to reproduce or transmit this work or portions thereof in any other form or by any other electronic or mechanical means, including any information storage or retrieval system, unless expressly permitted by federal copyright law. Address inquiries to Great Source Education Group, Inc., 181 Ballardvale Street, Wilmington, Massachusetts 01887.

Printed in the United States of America
International Standard Book Number: 0-669-49084-9
1 2 3 4 5 6 7 8 9—MZ—08 07 06 05 04 03 02

READERS AND REVIEWERS

Jay Amberg
Glenbrook High School
Glenview, Illinois

Mary Baker
Beach Middle School
Chelsea, Michigan

Marlene Beirle
Westerville City Schools
Westerville, Ohio

Ann Bender
Guoin Creek Middle School
Speedway, Indiana

Martha Clarke
Roosevelt Center-Dayton
   Public Schools
Dayton, Ohio

Cindy Crandall
Suttons Bay Middle School
Suttons Bay, Michigan

Janet Crews
Wydown Middle School
Clayton, Missouri

Marilyn Crow
Wilmette Public Schools
Wilmette, Illinois

Deanna Day
Tucson, Arizona

Demetra Disotuar
Martin Luther King
   Lab School
Evanston, Illinois

Pam Embler
Allen Jay Middle School
High Point, North Carolina

Julie Engstrom
Hillside Junior High School
Boise, Idaho

Shelly Fabozzi
Holmes Middle School
Colorado Springs, Colorado

Aimee Freed
Perry Middle School
Worthington, Ohio

Patricia Fry
Templeton Middle School
Sussex, Wisconsin

Barb Furrer
Templeton Middle School
Sussex, Wisconsin

Lorraine Gerhart
Crivitz, Wisconsin

Laurie Goodman
Pioneer Middle School
Hanford, California

Jane Goodson
Brunswick, Georgia

Pam Grabman
Center Middle School
Youngstown, Ohio

Bianca Griffin
Audubon Middle School
Milwaukee, Wisconsin

Dorsey Hammond
Oakland University
Rochester, Michigan

Cheryl Harry
Southfield, Michigan

Jeff Hicks
Whitford Middle School
Beaverton, Oregon

Claire Hiller
Timber Ridge Magnet School
Skokie, Illinois

Terri Huck
John Bullen Accelerated
   Middle School
Kenosha, Wisconsin

Ralph Huhn, Jr.
Key West, Florida

Dana Humphrey
F. Zumwalt North
   Middle School
O'Fallon, Missouri

Dennis Jackson
Danvers Public Schools
Danvers, Massachusetts

Jean Lifford
Dedham High School
Dedham, Massachusetts

Linda Maloney
Ridgewood Junior
   High School
Arnold, Missouri

Nancy McEvoy
Anderson Middle School
Berkley, Michigan

Mary McHugh
Franklin School
Belleville, Illinois

Catherine McNary
Proviso West High School
Hillside, Illinois

Marsha Nadasky
Western Reserve
   Middle School
Berlin Center, Ohio

Cheryl Nuciforo
City School District of Troy
Troy, New York

Lucretia Pannozzo
John Jay Middle School
Katonah, New York

Brenda Peterson
Templeton Middle School
Sussex, Wisconsin

Evelyn Price
Grand Avenue Middle School
Milwaukee, Wisconsin

Richard Santeusanio
Danvers School District
Danvers, Massachusetts

Jennifer Sellenriek
Wydown Middle School
Clayton, Missouri

Jill Vavrek
Proviso West High School
Hillside, Illinois

Dave Wendelin
Educational Service Center
Golden, Colorado

Michel Wendell
Archdiocese of St. Louis
   Cathedral School
St. Louis, Missouri

Roberta Williams
Traverse City East Junior
   High School
Traverse City, Michigan

Sharon Williams
Bay Point Middle School
St. Petersburg, Florida

Table of Contents

Lesson Plan Book Overview

The *Lesson Plan Book* includes a suggested reading curriculum for each grade level, weekly and daily lesson plans, and professional articles.

Week at a Glance

Shows **daily lessons** for the week.

Summary notes can be used to teach mini-lessons.

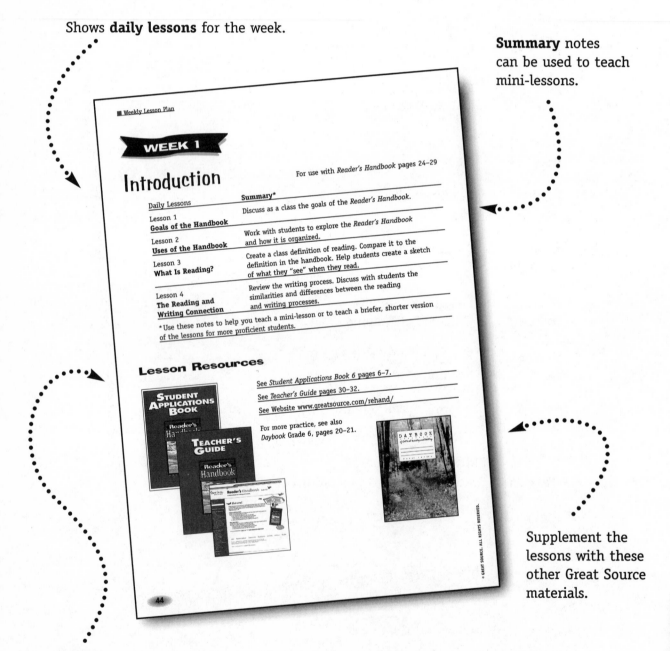

■ Weekly Lesson Plan

WEEK 1

Introduction

For use with *Reader's Handbook* pages 24–29

Daily Lessons	Summary*
Lesson 1 **Goals of the Handbook**	Discuss as a class the goals of the *Reader's Handbook*.
Lesson 2 **Uses of the Handbook**	Work with students to explore the *Reader's Handbook* and how it is organized.
Lesson 3 **What Is Reading?**	Create a class definition of reading. Compare it to the definition in the handbook. Help students create a sketch of what they "see" when they read.
Lesson 4 **The Reading and Writing Connection**	Review the writing process. Discuss with students the similarities and differences between the reading and writing processes.

*Use these notes to help you teach a mini-lesson or to teach a briefer, shorter version of the lessons for more proficient students.

Lesson Resources

See *Student Applications Book 6* pages 6–7.

See *Teacher's Guide* pages 30–32.

See Website www.greatsource.com/rehand/

For more practice, see also *Daybook* Grade 6, pages 20–21.

44

© GREAT SOURCE. ALL RIGHTS RESERVED.

Supplement the lessons with these other Great Source materials.

The **Lesson Resources** show all of the other materials that accompany the lesson.

Lesson Plans

Each daily lesson begins with a **Goal.**

The **Teaching Focus** section gives background along with key instruction.

∎ Daily Lesson Plan

WEEK 1
Lesson 1   Goals of the Handbook

For use with *Reader's Handbook* pages 14–15

Goals

In this introductory lesson, students learn three main goals of the handbook.

Teaching Focus

Background
Explain the importance of learning what you need to learn. Goals give a journey, a place to point toward. By understanding the goals of the handbook, students will find their learning becomes easier.

Instruction
Help students to understand the importance of having good models, good strategies, and a wide understanding of different kinds of readings. Use an analogy to something in the students' world, like modeling how to bat and field in baseball. Students see how to do something when they see it modeled. Then, they need to learn technique—a way to coil, bend at the knees, hold the bat, and so on. Last, they need to understand the nuances of how to handle different kinds of pitches as a batter. Explain to students that they learn to read the same way.

Either in small groups or as a whole class, discuss with students ways they have learned how to do something and the ways that worked best for them.

Teaching Approach

Use of the Handbook
Ask student volunteers to read through the Goals on pages 14–15. Then discuss which of the goals seems most important to them, and discuss the reasons why. Help students see that all of the goals are important.

Extend the Handbook
Introduce the idea of the handbook goals to the whole class. Then ask students to work in pairs to explore what modeling, learning strategies, and learning about kinds of readings mean. Let students explain to each other why modeling good reading habits will be important and what they mean by using "reading strategies."

Assessment
Ask students:

∎ What are you supposed to learn from the *Reader's Handbook*?

∎ Why is having a model of how to do something important?

∎ When have you used models in other things you do?

∎ What kinds of reading strategies do you now use? Do you know enough of them?

∎ What sorts of materials do you read, and do you feel prepared to read all of them?

46

The **Teaching Approach** shows how to use and extend the handbook with the lesson, as well as ways to assess student learning.

Frequently Asked Questions

How did you define what a reading strategy is, and how did you choose which ones to use in the handbook?

In the *Reader's Handbook*, a **strategy** is defined as having a broad application across different genres. A strategy can serve a number of purposes. For example, you can *outline* or *find cause and effect* with fiction or nonfiction, a textbook, or a test. But some skills, such as *drawing conclusions* or *comparing and contrasting,* are so fundamental that they underlie almost everything. That's why these skills are called **"reading know-how."** The handbook also refers to **"reading tools,"** which are more specialized and have a specific use or purpose. The Almanac lists 36 key reading tools used throughout the handbook. A K-W-L Chart, for example, is used with nonfiction texts; Story Strings work specifically with fiction; Two Per Line is most appropriate for poetry. These distinctions between strategies, know-how, and tools are an attempt to use terms consistently in the absence of any consensus and an attempt to create a set of terms teachers can use within a school to create a shared, common language.

How did you decide on these specific steps of the reading process, and why are they in the order they are?

Reading is almost infinitely complex. It—like writing—hardly follows any single process or, for that matter, works in any single direction. But students need specifics on what to do. They need a good model, and they need to develop good habits. So, rather than presenting reading in all its complex splendor, the handbook organizes reading around an easy-to-remember process, explaining what students need to do Before, During, and After Reading. It breaks down the process into brief, easy steps. As with the writing process, students may sometimes skip a step, go backward occasionally, or spend a long time on one of the steps. That's OK. The reading process will help students make the decisions they need in order to be effective readers.

What kind of students is the handbook for?

The *Reader's Handbook* is for all students. Different students will take away different things from the handbook. Good readers will refine the strategies they use and learn some new reading tools they can apply, and perhaps even learn more about how different kinds of texts are organized. Average readers will add to the reading strategies and tools they use, and they'll develop a stronger understanding of the reading process. And students who struggle will acquire some good strategies, tools, and understanding of the process of reading.

Where should I begin as a teacher?

For help in teaching the handbook, start with the *Teacher's Guide* and *Overhead Transparencies*. To develop a curriculum or daily lesson plans, start with the *Lesson Plan Book* for your grade. To see if students can apply the strategies, use the *Student Applications Book* for your grade.

For more Frequently Asked Questions, see the website at www.greatsource.com/rehand/

Reading Curriculum

Each *Lesson Plan Book* suggests a reading curriculum for teachers to implement in their classrooms. This curriculum was designed for a 36-week school year, and it shows what a teacher can reasonably cover in a single year. For convenience, the *Lesson Plan Book* organized lesson plans in two-week segments, so you can see at a glance all of the daily lessons and resources for a genre.

To customize a curriculum for your students, see pages 12–15.

Grade 6 Curriculum

Week	Unit	Week	Unit
1	Introduction	19	Reading a Novel
2	The Reading Process	20	Reading a Novel
3	Essential Reading Skills	21	Elements of Fiction
4	Reading Actively	22	Elements of Fiction
5	Reading Know-how: Reading Paragraphs	23	Reading a Poem
6	Reading Know-how: Reading Paragraphs	24	Elements of Poetry
7	Reading Geography	25	Reading a Play
8	Reading Geography	26	Focus on Language
9	Elements of Textbooks	27	Reading a Website
10	Elements of Nonfiction	28	Elements of the Internet
11	Reading Biographies and Autobiographies	29	Reading a Graphic
12	Reading Biographies and Autobiographies	30	Elements of Graphics
13	Reading a Newspaper Article	31	Reading a Test and Test Questions
14	Focus on Persuasive Writing	32	Reading a Test and Test Questions
15	Reading a Short Story	33	Improving Vocabulary
16	Focus on Plot	34	Improving Vocabulary
17	Focus on Characters	35	Strategy Handbook
18	Focus on Setting	36	Reading Tools

Grade 7 Curriculum

<table>
<tr><td>Week</td><td>Unit</td><td>Week</td><td>Unit</td></tr>
<tr><td>1</td><td>Introduction</td><td>19</td><td>Elements of Fiction</td></tr>
<tr><td>2</td><td>The Reading Process</td><td>20</td><td>Elements of Poetry</td></tr>
<tr><td>3</td><td>Reading Know-how</td><td>21</td><td>Reading a Poem</td></tr>
<tr><td>4</td><td>Reading Paragraphs</td><td>22</td><td>Focus on Language</td></tr>
<tr><td>5</td><td>Reading History</td><td>23</td><td>Reading a Play</td></tr>
<tr><td>6</td><td>Reading History</td><td>24</td><td>Elements of Drama</td></tr>
<tr><td>7</td><td>Reading Math</td><td>25</td><td>Reading a Website</td></tr>
<tr><td>8</td><td>Focus on Word Problems</td><td>26</td><td>Elements of the Internet</td></tr>
<tr><td>9</td><td>Elements of Textbooks</td><td>27</td><td>Reading a Graphic</td></tr>
<tr><td>10</td><td>Elements of Nonfiction</td><td>28</td><td>Elements of Graphics</td></tr>
<tr><td>11</td><td>Reading an Essay</td><td>29</td><td>Reading a Test and Test Questions</td></tr>
<tr><td>12</td><td>Reading an Essay</td><td>30</td><td>Focus on Essay Tests</td></tr>
<tr><td>13</td><td>Reading a Magazine Article</td><td>31</td><td>Focus on Math Tests</td></tr>
<tr><td>14</td><td>Focus on Speeches</td><td>32</td><td>Focus on Science Tests</td></tr>
<tr><td>15</td><td>Reading a Short Story</td><td>33</td><td>Improving Vocabulary</td></tr>
<tr><td>16</td><td>Reading a Novel</td><td>34</td><td>Improving Vocabulary</td></tr>
<tr><td>17</td><td>Focus on Dialogue</td><td>35</td><td>The Reader's Almanac</td></tr>
<tr><td>18</td><td>Focus on Theme</td><td>36</td><td>The Reader's Almanac</td></tr>
</table>

Grade 8 Curriculum

Week	Unit
1	Introduction
2	The Reading Process
3	Reading Know-how
4	Reading History
5	Reading Science
6	Reading Science
7	Reading Math
8	Elements of Textbooks
9	Reading an Essay
10	Reading Biographies and Autobiographies
11	Reading a Magazine Article
12	Focus on Persuasive Writing
13	Focus on Real-world Writing
14	Elements of Nonfiction
15	Reading a Short Story
16	Reading a Novel
17	Focus on Plot and Theme
18	Focus on Comparing and Contrasting

Week	Unit
19	Elements of Fiction
20	Elements of Poetry
21	Reading a Poem
22	Focus on Meaning, Sound, & Structure
23	Reading a Play
24	Focus on Theme and Language
25	Reading a Website
26	Reading a Graphic
27	Reading a Test and Test Questions
28	Focus on Essay Tests
29	Focus on Vocabulary Tests
30	Focus on Social Studies Tests
31	Focus on Math Tests
32	Focus on Science Tests
33	Improving Vocabulary
34	Improving Vocabulary
35	The Reader's Almanac
36	The Reader's Almanac

Build Your Own Curriculum

The lesson plans in the *Lesson Plan Book* are adaptable to fit any curriculum. You can pick and choose lessons to teach with a specific emphasis. You can also use lesson plans from other grade levels, which are available from the website (www.greatsource.com/rehand/). See the examples below and on the next page for suggestions to design your own curriculum.

Example

Use the year-long Curriculum Plan to map out which chapters to teach in each quarter. The example below shows a model that emphasizes teaching reading across the curriculum.

Reading Across the Curriculum Focus

Quarter 1	Quarter 2
Reading Process Reading Know-how Reading Textbooks	Reading Textbooks Reading Nonfiction
Quarter 3	**Quarter 4**
Reading Fiction Reading Poetry Reading Graphics	Reading Drama Reading on the Internet Reading for Tests Improving Vocabulary

Quarter 1 Plan

Week 1	Reading Process
Week 2	Reading Know-how
Week 3	Reading Know-how
Week 4	Elements of Textbooks
Week 5	Reading History
Week 6	Reading Geography
Week 7	Reading Science
Week 8	Reading Science
Week 9	Reading History

Once a Curriculum Plan is set for the year, create a Quarter Plan to focus on which lessons to teach week by week during each quarter.

Other Year-long Curriculum Plan Examples

Vocabulary and Language Focus

Quarter 1	Quarter 2
Reading Process Reading Know-how Improving Vocabulary Reading Textbooks	Reading Fiction Reading Poetry Reading Nonfiction Reading for Tests
Quarter 3	**Quarter 4**
Reading Textbooks Reading Nonfiction Reading Poetry Improving Vocabulary	Reading Graphics Reading Drama Improving Vocabulary Reading for Tests

Literature Focus

Quarter 1	Quarter 2
Reading Process Reading Know-how Improving Vocabulary Reading Fiction	Reading Fiction Reading Poetry Improving Vocabulary Reading for Tests
Quarter 3	**Quarter 4**
Reading Textbooks Reading Nonfiction Reading Drama Reading Poetry	Reading Nonfiction Reading Graphics Reading on the Internet Reading for Tests

Test-Success Focus

Quarter 1	Quarter 2
Reading Process Reading Know-how Improving Vocabulary Reading for Tests	Reading Textbooks Reading Graphics Reading Nonfiction Reading for Tests
Quarter 3	**Quarter 4**
Reading Fiction Reading Poetry Improving Vocabulary Reading for Tests	Reading Drama Reading on the Internet Reading Textbooks Reading for Tests

Build Your Own Curriculum

CURRICULUM:_____

1st Quarter	2nd Quarter
....	....
....	....
....	....
....	....
....	....
....	....
....	....
3rd Quarter	**4th Quarter**
....	....
....	....
....	....
....	....
....	....
....	....
....	....

Build Your Own Curriculum

QUARTER:_____

Week 1 _____

Week 2 _____

Week 3 _____

Week 4 _____

Week 5 _____

Week 6 _____

Week 7 _____

Week 8 _____

Week 9 _____

Reading Strategy Overview

Reading Lesson	Selection	Reading Strategy	Rereading Strategy
Reading History	"Indian Wars"	Note-taking	Outlining
Reading Geography	"Population"	Using Graphic Organizers	Note-taking
Reading Science	"Exploring the Ocean"	Note-taking	Skimming
Reading Math	"Connections to Algebra"	Visualizing and Thinking Aloud	Note-taking
Reading an Essay	"America the Not-so-Beautiful"	Outlining	Questioning the Author
Reading a Biography	*Harriet Tubman: Conductor on the Underground Railroad*	Looking for Cause and Effect	Outlining
Reading an Autobiography	*Up from Slavery*	Synthesizing	Looking for Cause and Effect
Reading a Newspaper Article	"Robots get ready to rumble"	Reading Critically	Summarizing
Reading a Magazine Article	"A Killer Gets Some Respect"	Questioning the Author	Reading Critically
Reading a Short Story	"Charles"	Using Graphic Organizers	Close Reading
Reading a Novel	*Roll of Thunder, Hear My Cry*	Synthesizing	Using Graphic Organizers
Reading a Poem	"Winter Poem"	Close Reading	Paraphrasing
Reading a Play	*The Diary of Anne Frank*	Summarizing	Visualizing and Thinking Aloud
Reading a Website	The International Dyslexia Association Website	Reading Critically	Skimming
Reading a Graphic	"Gallup Survey on Crime"	Paraphrasing	Reading Critically
Reading a Test and Test Questions	*Geronimo: His Own Story*	Skimming	Visualizing and Thinking Aloud

Focus Lesson	Selection	Reading Strategy
Focus on Science Concepts	"Cell Growth and Division"	Using Graphic Organizers
Focus on Word Problems	Math Problems	Visualizing and Thinking Aloud
Focus on Persuasive Writing	"Parents, Not Cash, Can Enrich a School"	Reading Critically
Focus on Speeches	"The future doesn't belong to the fainthearted"	Reading Critically
Focus on Real-world Writing	School Conduct Handbook Computer Game Instructions Train Schedule	Skimming
Focus on Characters	*The Cay*	Using Graphic Organizers
Focus on Setting	*Shiloh*	Close Reading
Focus on Dialogue	*Roll of Thunder, Hear My Cry*	Close Reading
Focus on Plot	"Last Cover"	Using Graphic Organizers
Focus on Theme	*Roll of Thunder, Hear My Cry*	
Focus on Comparing and Contrasting	Greek Myth of King Midas and *A Christmas Carol*	Using Graphic Organizers
Focus on Language	"Words"	Close Reading
Focus on Meaning	"Those Winter Sundays"	Close Reading
Focus on Sound and Structure	"The Sloth"	Close Reading
Focus on Theme	*The Diary of Anne Frank*	
Focus on Language	*The Diary of Anne Frank*	
Focus on Essay Tests	Sample Essay Questions	
Focus on Vocabulary Tests	Sample Vocabulary Questions	
Focus on Social Studies Tests	Sample Social Studies Questions	
Focus on Math Tests	Sample Math Questions	
Focus on Science Tests	Sample Science Questions	

Guide to the *Reader's Handbook*

Reading Lessons

Reading lessons model how to read different kinds of materials using the reading process. The reading process has three steps: Before Reading, During Reading, and After Reading.

Before Reading

Before Reading consists of setting a purpose, previewing a reading, and planning a reading strategy.

The Goals box shows **what students will learn** from the lesson.

Goals

Here you'll learn how to:

- ✔ read **history**
- ✔ use the strategy of **note-taking**
- ✔ see **the way history textbooks are often organized**

The Setting a Purpose box suggests one or more **questions that students can attempt to answer as they read.**

Setting a Purpose

- ■ **What** were the Indian Wars?
- ■ **When** did they take place?
- ■ **Who** was involved in these wars?
- ■ **Where** did they take place?
- ■ **Why** did they occur?

The Preview Checklist lists what to look for when **previewing a reading.**

Preview Checklist

- ✔ the title and any section guides or goals boxes
- ✔ the first and last paragraphs
- ✔ the headings
- ✔ any names, dates, words, or terms set in boldface or that are repeated
- ✔ any photos, diagrams, or pictures and their captions

The Reading Strategy helps students **use a reading strategy** for a specific type of reading.

Reading Strategy: Note-taking

So, here's your purpose—to gather general, basic information about the Indian Wars. One excellent strategy to use to collect that information is **note-taking.**

During Reading

The During Reading step includes reading actively, looking for information that fits the reading purpose, and creating a personal connection to the text.

Reading Tools are suggested to help students understand the reading and **look for information that fits their reading purpose.**

1. Summary Notes

Learn something from each page or section of your textbook. Take notes about the most important information. Look for key facts or names and any terms or ideas in boldface or headings.

> **Page 559**
>
> 1800—Indians lived in peace.
> 1840—Reservations began.
> Indians and whites clashed on Plains.

> **Page 560**
>
> 1860s—Treaties were broken.
> Settlers went through Indian lands and killed buffalo. Indians raided white settlements.

> **Page 561**
>
> 1876—Sitting Bull and Crazy Horse attacked Gen. Custer. Massacre was last major Indian victory.

The How Texts Are Organized **looks at how different kinds of reading are organized** so students can understand them better.

How History Textbooks Are Organized

Active readers can create more understanding than readers who simply turn the pages. Understanding a passage takes time and effort, and it helps to know the kinds of things to look for.

Look back for a moment at the history text on pages 69–72. If you follow the highlighting in the example, you will notice that the reader marked many of the names, dates, and locations. History textbooks like this one often follow **time** (or chronological) **order.**

Dates—Time Order

Locations— Geographic Order

In the Connect step, students **create a personal connection to the text.**

Connect

The idea that you are responsible for your own reading is one of the most important ideas in this handbook. You need to take charge and grab the information you need.

After Reading

The After Reading step includes pausing, reflecting, and looking back to see if students accomplished their reading purpose. It also shows students a rereading strategy to find information they may have missed the first time around. The last part is Remember, a final step that suggests ways students can remember what they've learned.

The Looking Back checklist asks students to monitor their reading. This helps students see if they've **accomplished their reading purpose.**

Looking Back

- Can I answer the *who, what, where, when,* and *why* questions?
- Can I summarize 2–3 important ideas in my own words?
- Do my notes cover the whole chapter, and do I understand them?

A Rereading Strategy is suggested so students can **find out information they may have missed the first time through.**

Rereading Strategy: Outlining

When you reread, try a new reading strategy. **Outlining** is a good way to review the key information in a chapter. Remember when you previewed the headings? They can help you create a quick, effective Topic or Sentence Outline. Textbooks are usually carefully organized.

The Remember step shows one or more ways students can **remember what they've learned.**

1. Share Your Ideas
Talk about what you learned with a friend or family member. Find out what they know about the Indian Wars. Ask some of your classmates what they found most interesting or surprising. Getting into a conversation about what you read is a great way to remember more about it.

2. Create a Chart or Organizer
The act of creation helps you "make the material your own," and that helps you remember it. By creating some notes, a chart, or a graphic organizer, you give your brain a way to "see" the information you learned.

Focus Lessons

Focus lessons take a closer look at one type of reading or specific element, such as theme, setting, essay tests, and so on. They are shorter lessons that zero in on a single subject. A combination of reading tools, reading strategies, and tips is suggested to help students better understand the subject.

Elements Lessons

Elements lessons explain key terms related to the genre. Each lesson starts off with an **example,** so students see how the term is used. Next, students read a **description** about the term in the example. The lesson ends with a clear **definition**.

Reader's Almanac

The Reader's Almanac is a reference guide.

The **Strategy Handbook** describes in detail each of the 12 main reading strategies.

The **Reading Tools** section describes and gives examples of the 36 main reading tools.

Last, **Word Parts** gives a list of prefixes, suffixes, and roots.

Focus on Science Tests

Since much of the vocabulary in science is different from your everyday vocabulary, learning science sometimes seems like learning a whole new language. When you are preparing for science tests, spend time learning the language of science. You'll also need to think like a scientist and learn the scientific method.

Goals

Here you'll learn how to:
✓ prepare for science tests
✓ preview and work through test questions
✓ read science charts, tables, diagrams, and graphs

Before Reading

The time to start preparing for a science test is not the night before. It's every day. Make it a habit to read carefully the material assigned in your science texts. Next, try to learn basic science terms, such as *molecule, ecology, photosynthesis, virus,* and so on.

Learn to take science notes—on what you
read on your own. Predict
on what th

Elements of Textbooks

Glossary

All school subjects have their own specialized terms, and most textbooks list them in a glossary. It usually appears in the back of the textbook.

EXAMPLE

GLOSSARY

Key term in bold → **abolition** (a uh LIHSH uhn) n. the movement to end slavery. (p. 440)
abridge (uh BRIHJ) v. to reduce. (p. 266)
AEF n. the American Expeditionary Force, U.S. forces during World War I. (p. 686)
Definition or description → **affirmation** (af uhr MAY shuhn) n. a statement declaring that something is true. (p. 257)
African Diaspora (AF rih kuhn dy AS puhr uh) n. the forced removal of Africans from their homelands to serve as slave labor in the Americas. (p. 78)
Agent Orange n. a chemical that kills plants. (p. 843)
Albany Plan of Union n. the first formal proposal to unite the American colonies, put forth by Benjamin
Page where term is used → Franklin. (p. 149)

DESCRIPTION

The purpose of the **glossary** (like these Elements pages in this handbook) is to give you the specialized language of the subject. This vocabulary is usually vital for your understanding of the subject.

terms or specialized vocabulary words for a
in a chapter preview. Take time

Close Reading

DESCRIPTION

Close reading means reading word for word, sentence by sentence, or line by line. It is like putting one part of a reading under a microscope and studying how the words look, sound, and work together.

Close reading is a good strategy to use with shorter selections, such as poems or speeches, or with small parts of a longer work. Choose parts that you know are important to the meaning of the selection as a whole.

Using the Strategy

To do a close reading, first you'll need to read the selection slowly and carefully.

1. Select and Read Choose a key passage or a few lines. If you're allowed to write on the page, use a highlighter or pen to mark important words. If you can't write on the page, cut sticky notes into narrow strips and use these strips to mark important parts in the selection.

2. Analyze Then, look at each passage you chose word for word. Ask yourself questions like these:
■ Why did the writer use this particular word?
■ What does this mean?
■ Why is this important?
■ What's special or unusual about the words used here?
■ What do the words mean, but also what do they suggest?

By answering these questions, you'll figure out what the passage means.

Correlations

Overview

The *Reader's Handbook* is a multifaceted guide to reading, and it easily supplements several other Great Source reading and writing products. Use the correlations charts that follow to see how to complement lessons with different materials.

1. Daybooks of Critical Reading and Writing, grade 6

Like the *Reader's Handbook*, the *Daybooks* show students how to become active readers. The *Daybooks* complement the *Reader's Handbook* by offering further opportunities to practice using reading strategies and tools, as well as the reading process and reading know-how. The *Daybooks* have been correlated to the *Reader's Handbook* through the genre of the selections. In other words, nonfiction selections from the *Daybooks* are suggested for the Reading Nonfiction chapter in the handbook; poetry selections with Reading Poetry, and so on.

Reader's Handbook Chapter	*Daybook*, Grade 6	Pages
I. Introduction	*The Friendship*	20–21
II. The Reading Process	from *The Gold Cadillac*	14–15
	from an interview	22–23
III. Reading Know-how	from *Roll of Thunder, Hear My Cry*	10–12
	"All Summer in a Day"	26–31
	"It's All in How You Say It"	33–34
IV. Reading Textbooks	from *Green Planet Rescue*	96
	from *And Then There Was One*	116–119
	from *Experimenting with Inventions*	126–127
	from *World: Adventures in Time and Place*	130–134
	from *The Ancient Egyptians*	136–137
	from *Egyptian Pyramids*	139–141
V. Reading Nonfiction	"A Uniformly Good Idea"	88
	from "Robots Will Never Replace Humans"	93
	from Newbery acceptance speech	113–114
	from "A Personal Narrative"	121–122
	from *An Owl in the House*	123–124
	from *Can It Really Rain Frogs?*	144–145
	from *The Titanic*	148–152
	from *It's Our World, Too!*	155–157
	"Hearing the Sweetest Songs"	189–193

Daybook, grade 6, continued

2. Reading and Writing Sourcebooks, grade 6

One way the *Reader's Handbook* can be used is to help struggling readers. The *Sourcebooks* focus on struggling readers, teach a reading process and reading tools, and encourage students to become active readers. In these three ways, the *Sourcebooks* complement the *Reader's Handbook*. To facilitate using both programs, each *Sourcebook* selection has been correlated to an appropriate chapter in the *Reader's Handbook*.

Reader's Handbook Chapter	Sourcebook, grade 6	Pages
II. The Reading Process	"Father" from *Living up the Street*	12–21
III. Reading Know-how	"Mother" from *The Seventh Child*	22–30
	"Joshua" from *The Journal of Joshua Loper*	50–57
IV. Reading Textbooks	"The Great Whales"	32–39
	"Killer Whales"	40–48
	"Egyptian Mummies"	84–91
V. Reading Nonfiction	"Mummies"	92–100
	"A Better Life"	122–130
	"Jackie Robinson's First Game"	131–140
	"The Strangers Arrive"	142–151
	"The Great Moctezuma"	152–160
	"Buffalo Hunt" from *My Indian Boyhood*	202–212
	"The Sunflower Room" from *Remember My Name*	213–222
	"Milo" from *The Phantom Tollbooth*	224–230
	"Milo" from *The Phantom Tollbooth*	231–238
VI. Reading Fiction	"Cheating" from *Family Secrets*	75–82
	"The Man" from *Somewhere in the Darkness*	58–66
	"Summer Berries" from *Sweetgrass*	102–110
	"Summer Berries" from *Sweetgrass*	111–120
	"I am Miguel," from *. . . and now Miguel*	162–169
	"Sangre de Cristo Mountains" from *. . .and now Miguel*	170–180
	"Bradley Chalkers" from *There's a Boy in the Girls Bathroom*	182–189
XII. Improving Vocabulary	"What Happened During the Ice Storm"	68–74
	"Sam Gribley" from *On the Far Side of the Mountain*	190–200

3. Write Source 2000

The main goal of the *Reader's Handbook* is to teach all students how to become better readers. *Write Source 2000* directly complements the handbook through its teaching of a writing process and how types of writing are organized. To teach both programs side by side, the correlation below shows which parts of *Write Source 2000* best complement individual chapters in the *Reader's Handbook*.

Reader's Handbook Chapter	Correlation	*Write Source 2000* ©1999
I. Introduction	understanding writing	3–8
II. The Reading Process	writing process	5–18
III. Reading Know-how	writing paragraphs	56, 110, 310–311, 377
IV. Reading Textbooks	word problems	281, 301–306, 466–482,
	note-taking	491–506, 528
V. Reading Nonfiction	essays	56, 103, 115–122,
		170–173, 263
VI. Reading Fiction	novels	176, 184, 277, 294,
	stories	342, 343–344
VII. Reading Poetry	writing a poem	193–207, 342
VIII. Reading Drama	writing a play	342
IX. Reading on the Internet	using the Internet	43, 265–272
X. Reading Graphics	using graphs	56, 302–303
XI. Reading for Tests	test-taking skills	375–380
XII. Improving Vocabulary	improving vocabulary	323–340

The Place of Reading in Middle School

by Jolene Borgese and Wendell Schwartz

Why teach reading in middle school?

For many of us, the teaching of reading beyond the third or fourth grade seems like the mythical Gordian knot. As teachers, all too often we are not sure where to begin. Oddly enough, when confronting an obviously struggling reader, teachers may have numerous resources, such as remedial reading classes, reading specialists, or even tutors available. However, as the reader's abilities improve and decoding is no longer a problem, the issues become more subtle and the solutions to the student's needs are less obvious. As teachers, we all know that reading is a skill that continues to grow and mature all through our lives and that our students, even the successful ones, can become more efficient and effective readers only if we better understand how we can help them grow.

How well can students read?

A popular rallying cry in recent years has been that "All teachers are teachers of reading." But, especially in middle school and high school, where teachers are often subject area specialists, that simply is not true; we are teachers of science, of math, of literature, of history. Most of us do not define ourselves as teachers of reading; if we do at all, it is usually a secondary role. According to Ruth Schoenbach in *Reading for Understanding*, "Many middle school teachers and most high school teachers see their primary responsibility as teaching the important knowledge base of their disciplines—the content. Filling in orally what students are either not able or not willing to learn from the course texts is a natural response for any dedicated teacher. . . . Teachers may read to students, talk through the book, or show a related video." Rather than helping our students to read the text, we find ways to work around the reading act in an effort to help our students learn the content. This points to the clear need for a reading program that is rooted in the various content areas of the middle school curriculum and that has as its goal the improved learning and achievement of the students in each subject area. We all know that our students need to be effective readers in order to succeed in our classrooms and, in fact, long after that.

Very often it seems that we understand what to do at the beginning of the reading process. For example, beginning a piece of fiction for most students is like the prewriting activities we ask them to do before they write. This is usually the fun part— previewing, predicting, and building interest. These are usually activities students can do without much stress. Teachers have a long history of knowing how to check for comprehension. Short quizzes, extensive essay exams, classroom discussions, book reports, oral presentations, and objective tests all are tools we use to check for understanding after the reading is completed.

However, so many of these post–reading assessments reveal that students' reading has been ineffective. Something has gone wrong during the reading process, and we now find ourselves at a loss on what to do. While a teacher can look at an early draft of a student's writing and understand what happened during the writing process, the during reading step of the reading process cannot be seen. It is at this point that we as teachers should see the need to teach more reading skills and strategies that will help our students monitor their own understanding and to take these skills and transfer them to other reading experiences.

What are the characteristics of the middle school reader?

Think about the students who fill your classrooms every day, year after year. Chances are good that they will fall into at least a few broad, general classifications. There will be those who clearly are struggling to keep up with their peers. These students may put forth effort and read the assignments we give them, but all too often we hear from them the familiar refrain, "I read it, but I didn't get it." This is probably true in many, many cases. They know the words, but they don't really know how to read in the truest sense of the word.

According to Ruth Schoenbach in *Reading for Understanding*, "Most adolescents whom teachers might initially describe as 'not even able to get the words off the page' are far less likely to have problems with decoding than with comprehension, unfamiliar vocabulary, insufficient background knowledge, reading fluency, or engagement."

At the opposite end of the spectrum are those students who are skillful readers. They interact with the text, often without realizing it. They ask themselves questions as they read, monitor their comprehension, and make adjustments along the way. They anticipate what may happen next in a story or what the author's intent or purpose in an article may be. They have strategies for integrating new knowledge into what they already understand, and when that does not happen, they know what questions to ask.

For example, in *Reading Reminders*, Jim Burke writes about teaching his students to ask themselves questions not only after they read, but while they read as well. This leads to what Burke calls "dense" questions that help them to relate what they have read to other things they have read, to other things in their experience, and to what they may already know about the topic. These students read with insight and with understanding. They have a general sense, sometimes almost innate, of the reading process. And, they read with a purpose.

What if my students can already read?

But most students probably fall somewhere between these two extremes. They read some texts more successfully than others, often because they have a limited number of techniques or strategies, and they tend to read all texts the same way. A short story is approached in much the same way a chapter in a science book is approached. They do not monitor their own comprehension during the actual act of reading, deciding—when it's too late—that they didn't understand important elements of the text but not knowing what to do about it "after the fact." They may have a sense of the reading process, but it is only vaguely defined for them. They may understand what to do at the beginning of a reading task, but they do not know what to do as they are reading or what to do after they have finished.

Many of us would define these students as "about average" readers, when in fact they are not really readers at all. They often find ways to compensate for limited reading skills and for barely finishing their reading assignments (if at all). They may be good listeners in class; they may be good at studying for tests, even though they understood only some of what they read along the way. These students present us, as teachers, with the greatest challenges because they are not usually thought of as students with "reading problems," yet when asked to read and comprehend on their own, their success is limited.

What's the current state of middle school reading programs?

In recent years, the specific reading curriculum—that is, a coherent, sequenced series of competencies and skills embedded in a meaningful context—has slipped away. Teachers are exhorted to make their students better readers, but given little support, inservice, or materials to help them achieve this goal. Teachers find themselves left to their own resources to try to figure out "what works," and that usually is some variation of what has worked for them over the years. There are few, if any, formal reading programs currently in place for use in the middle school. Generally, reading programs are seen as appropriate for the lower elementary grades, and as long as students know how to decode the words in front of them, "reading" is taking place as best it can with our older students.

In most middle schools, the reading of various forms of literature takes the place of actual reading instruction. Teachers may try to help students in these "reading" classes, but most often the goal is to help students understand the story, essay, or poem, not to consciously employ reading strategies that will help them later when they encounter challenging texts on their own. Where formal reading programs do exist, they are usually created with the weak or struggling reader in mind. Thus, the direct teaching of reading at the middle or high school level becomes a "remedial" issue, where poor students are "fixed" in hopes that their learning will eventually improve. Reading programs for successful or even moderately able students do not exist in most places. As Ruth Schoenbach says in *Reading for Understanding,* "The idea that at age eleven, fourteen, or seventeen it is too late to become a strong and independent reader of academic texts is both insidious and self-perpetuating. . . . The assumption that children who have not become good readers in the early grades will never catch up is both incorrect and destructive."

How can you teach reading?

For many of us in the classroom, the direct teaching of reading was not part of our teacher training. We were taught how to encourage, how to coach, how to support students as they try to master our various content areas. We were not taught, however, how to demonstrate, model, and present specific reading techniques and strategies that would help all of our students, the weak readers as well as the strong ones, to become better students and to achieve at higher levels.

What's the *Reader's Handbook* solution?

The *Reader's Handbook* is designed to be used by students at all these levels of reading proficiency. It will be useful for struggling readers by introducing them to the reading process, the central concept of all effective reading. It will help them to set a purpose for their reading beyond simply finishing it. The *Reader's Handbook* will help them to learn how to answer questions as they read, not only after they have finished. It will help them learn how to reflect on what they have read and decide what to do next. As most teachers know, these are skills that struggling readers simply do not have. There are also strategies and tools for dealing with vocabulary issues, for taking notes, and for using graphic organizers. The *Reader's Handbook* also contains dozens of other comprehension aids that struggling or reluctant readers either know nothing at all about or are seldom called upon to use.

Just as important, the *Reader's Handbook* can help proficient and highly skillful readers become even better. Reading is a skill for which there is really no "ceiling," and the *Reader's Handbook* can help these readers address issues of academic literacy that will increase their levels of achievement in all content areas. The handbook includes suggestions for learning how to synthesize information that is often presented in different formats— for example, traditional text combined with graphs or illustrations. The *Reader's Handbook* presents many ways for self-monitoring of comprehension during the act of reading itself. Specific approaches to the reading of various genres of literature, as well as textbooks and other types of nonfiction, are also addressed.

For the more skillful readers, the handbook discusses typical text structures they can expect to encounter and how to deal with them effectively and efficiently. A conscious understanding of the most prevalent text structures and how information is embedded within them is a sophisticated skill that good middle school readers seldom can articulate. Reading non-traditional material, such as websites and graphics, is also thoroughly covered. Even tailoring how one reads various kinds of tests is presented.

In short, the *Reader's Handbook* is not simply a "remedial" book for struggling readers. It is a book that can and does introduce weak readers to critical strategies and tools that will help them improve their comprehension. But it can also assist proficient readers to become more purposeful in their approach to a multitude of reading tasks and become more successful in all areas of the curriculum as a result.

How would I use the *Reader's Handbook?*

From a teacher's perspective, the *Reader's Handbook* can be used in several ways. Perhaps the single most important issue to understand is that it is intended to be useful and supportive for teachers in all content areas, not only reading. The *Reader's Handbook* needs to be viewed as a resource to be used by students in all of their classes. As the table of contents reveals, there are very specific sections of the handbook dedicated to reading strategies in specific areas of the middle school curriculum, from literature in its various forms, to reading in math class, social studies, science, and more. In some schools, the *Reader's Handbook* may become the backbone of a school-wide reading program covering grades 6–8. Together with its enrichment materials, it is extensive and versatile enough to provide instructional units for all levels of readers over a period of years.

In other cases, the *Reader's Handbook* may be seen as exactly that, a handbook. A teacher can use it contextually and as an integral part of preparing his or her students for an important upcoming reading task. For example, at the beginning of the school year, the social studies teacher will want to use the handbook as a guide for showing his or her students how to most effectively deal with the many elements of the typical history textbook. Later in the school year, that same teacher may call on the handbook again for lessons on how to read graphs, charts, and illustrations. Finally, before the students are asked to go the library to gather information, the unit on reading a website would be of great help.

Teachers may rely on the *Reader's Handbook* to provide them not only with the skeleton of a coherent reading program, but also with enough material to flesh out the program as well. Others may see it primarily as a book a teacher "dips into" to troubleshoot reading issues as they are identified to prepare his or her students for a challenging or new kind of reading. The *Reader's Handbook* is a resource for teachers and students that has many uses, the chief of which is to make students better readers.

REFERENCES

Burke, J. (2000). *Reading reminders: tools, tips, and techniques.* Portsmouth: Boynton/Cook Heinemann.

Robb, L. (2000). *Teaching reading in middle school.* New York: Scholastic.

Schoenbach, R., et al. (1999). *Reading for understanding.* San Francisco: Jossey-Bass.

Teaching a Reading and Writing Workshop

by Laura Robb

"I like all the different things we do in workshop—read, discuss, write, work with a partner or our teacher. And most of the time I'm liking what we do." These words, spoken by a sixth-grade boy, say a great deal about the varied learning experiences in a reading workshop. Within a block of time, a workshop approach to reading enables you to model reading strategies, then support individuals and small groups, while the rest of the class completes independent reading, discusses a text, or writes about their reading.

The Benefits of a Reading/Writing Workshop

- **Independence** Middle school students can develop the independence they crave during choice time when students work alone, in pairs, or in small groups.

- **Guided Practice** The blocks of time available during a workshop allow students to practice and apply strategies and skills to new materials under the expert guidance of you, the teacher.

- **Social Aspects of Learning** Talking to and hanging out with friends is what middle schoolers enjoy. Workshops build on students' social natures by fostering focused talk about reading.

- **Flexible Grouping** Because students learn to work independently, teachers can meet with individuals or small groups to support strategic reading and the interpretation of various literary genres.

Establish Workshop Routines

Reflect on the kinds of independent work you want students to complete during the workshop. Here's the list a seventh-grade teacher compiled: independent reading; reviewing specific genres in the *Reader's Handbook*; applying reading methods such as marking the text, finding the main idea, using a graphic organizer to figure out theme in their independent reading books; or completing a lesson in the *Daybook* or *Sourcebook* that relates to what's being studied in the *Reader's Handbook*.

Allow five to six weeks to teach routines and have students practice them, as well as understand what the behavior expectations are. The time you invest in helping students understand the different levels of workshop learning is directly related to the level of organization and productivity in your class.

Four Workshop Elements

The graphic organizer on page 34 will help you visualize these workshop elements.

1. Teach It By planning a mini-lesson, you can demonstrate how a reading or writing strategy works for you by modeling your process and thinking aloud to share your anxieties, frustrations, and ideas. The *Reader's Handbook* offers a wealth of mini-lesson ideas. Start the year by presenting these mini-lessons from the *Reader's Handbook*: "The Reading Process" and "Reading Know-how." You'll also want to design and present these mini-lessons: "Reading Nonfiction," "Reading Fiction," "Reading Poetry," "Reading Drama," "Reading for Tests," and "Improving Vocabulary." One possible curriculum to follow is laid out in the *Lesson Plan Book*. Use it as a model to construct your own, or follow it as a plan for your school.

2. Practice It During this block of time, you can work with groups who need support with applying strategies to different materials. While you work with a small group, student-led groups or partners can discuss literature, write about their reading, read independently, or study and review specific pages in the *Reader's Handbook*. For example, if you've had two to three mini-lessons on the short story, you might want students to check the Reader's Almanac in their handbook for a refresher on Character Maps or Plot Diagrams.

3. Apply It Here students have multiple opportunities to work independently, with a partner or in a small group, to apply what they have learned and practiced to new material. You'll also be able to carve out some time during this block to support struggling readers or students who missed a lesson.

Once students have worked through the lesson on the novel in the *Reader's Handbook*, they can apply some of the strategies to a free-choice book at their independent reading level. Ask students to keep written work in their journals so that they have a record of their thinking and learning.

4. Evaluate It Student journals, independent work done in the *Student Applications Books*, and student's writing about literature are all potential assessments. Independently completed work in the *Daybooks* and *Sourcebooks* are also good assessments that you can use to evaluate students' progress.

While students complete work, you can block out some time to hold brief meetings with those who still need more guidance to improve their reading and writing skills.

Basic Workshop Experiences

The experiences that follow offer choices that enable you to interact with students and monitor their progress.

Teacher Read-Aloud Teachers read aloud from genres that relate to those the class is studying.

Paired Questioning Partners read passages and question one another.

Complete a Journal Entry See suggestions in the *Reader's Handbook* and *Student Applications Book*.

Practice a Strategy Students, solo or in small groups, use books at their independent reading level to cement their understanding of a strategy.

Peer Conferences Pairs or small groups discuss how they apply a reading strategy and/or share journal entries that explain a strategy. The *Teacher's Guide* offers a wealth of independent reading suggestions as well.

Student-led Book Discussions Organize heterogeneous groupings, mixing ability levels and gender. The *Reader's Handbook* offers many possible discussion topics: the structure of a genre and supporting examples from a text, finding themes, character analysis, cause and effect, close readings, inferences, and so on.

Teacher-led Strategic Reading Groups These are homogeneous pairs or small groups that require additional instruction on how to apply a reading strategy, complete a graphic organizer, or transfer their knowledge of a specific genre to students' independent reading.

Integrating the *Reader's Handbook* into Your Reading Workshop

Here are some suggestions for constructing strategy lessons and reading and writing experiences using the *Reader's Handbook*, the *Teacher's Guide,* and the *Student Applications Book*. As you integrate the *Reader's Handbook* into your workshop, you will discover dozens of additional learning experiences and strategy lessons to bring to your students.

Possible Mini-lessons

- Setting a purpose
- Reading autobiographies, biographies, essays, geography textbooks, history textbooks, magazine articles, math textbooks, newspaper articles, novels, science textbooks, short stories
- Previewing a text
- Making a reading plan
- Using graphic organizers
- Making connections
- Inferring ideas
- Understanding the structure of short stories, novels, poems
- Understanding the structure of nonfiction books, essays, newspapers

Guided Practice

- Use the *Student Applications Book* and offer opportunities to apply your mini-lessons during workshop time called "Practice It."
- Create reading and writing experiences from the *Reader's Handbook* and your *Lesson Plan Book,* such as taking notes, building vocabulary, and making personal connections.

Gathering Written Work for Evaluation

- Evaluate students' progress based on their journal writing.
- Collect work students complete in the *Student Applications Book,* and evaluate whether they understand a skill, tool, or strategy.

Independent Reading

- Reserve time for students to read books at their independent level.
- Invite students to choose books that relate to the genres you're teaching.

Sourcebooks and Daybooks

- Use *Sourcebooks* and *Daybooks* to engage students in practice and reinforcement at students' instructional levels. This means that in an eighth-grade class you might have students in a sixth-grade *Sourcebook* because they are reading at that level, students reading on grade level in an eighth-grade *Daybook,* and several in ninth- or tenth-grade *Daybooks* because they are proficient readers.
- If your class has many struggling readers, consider using the *Sourcebooks* to meet their needs. In such a sixth-grade class, most students will be in a fourth- or fifth-grade *Sourcebook.* Those reading on grade level will use a sixth-grade *Daybook.*

Closing Thoughts

As an indispensable resource for you and your students, the *Reader's Handbook* and support materials will quickly become the foundation for your workshop. By using these materials, you can organize a workshop that meets the needs of each child and reaches all reading levels.

REFERENCE
Robb, L. (2000). *Teaching reading in middle school.* New York: Scholastic.

Workshop Approach

Teach It
Model a strategy.
(10–20 minutes)

- Mini-lesson with *Reader's Handbook*
- At start, in middle
- Reading and/or writing strategy

Practice It
Students use; teacher supports.
(20–40 minutes)

- Discussion groups
- Strategic reading
- Groups—student and teacher led
- Writing
- Independent work

Reading/Writing Workshop

Apply It
Students refine reading and writing.
(15–30 minutes)

- Whole group, small group, independent
- Work with students who need extra help.
- Work with *Daybooks*, or *Sourcebooks*.

Evaluate It
Students show what they can do.
(15–30 minutes)

- Complete work independently.
- Write about reading and writing strategies.
- Teacher support for those who need help

34

Academic Literacy: Making Students Content Learners

by Ron Klemp

One of the challenges facing today's middle schools is the demand for rigorous demonstrations of competency across the curriculum. High-stakes testing has opened discussion surrounding middle school students' ability to successfully negotiate the demands of texts used in classrooms across every district in the United States. In order to accomplish deeper understanding across subject areas, teachers and students alike are having to gear up to the demands of academic literacy.

Academic literacy can be defined as a continuing developmental process of knowing how to navigate through different forms of text. Becoming academically literate means that a learner has an inventory of effective strategies to meet the demands of different forms of text. As students encounter graphics, attend to text structure, and handle new and somewhat perplexing vocabulary, they will need to use strategies that may not be a part of their past reading experiences. In addition, the emphasis on integration of a language arts curriculum across and through all disciplines has challenged secondary teachers to "think differently about the role of literacy in understanding content" (Irvin, 1998). Essentially, the challenge for teachers is to devise ways to support students' emergence into becoming academically literate.

A recent NAEP report (Campbell, et al., 1998) noted that many middle school students fail to understand texts beyond a literal level. On the surface, this report may be startling. But on a deeper level this revelation is not surprising. Many teachers and older students reveal that in their middle school experiences they were rarely asked to do more than report what was read in the text or what was said during the teacher's lecture. Most adults admit to their own middle school student careers being the same. The teacher lectured and students took notes or read chapters and then reported the information back to the teacher in the form of a test, quiz, or essay. The need for academic literacy did not extend very far. In addition, the report noted that most middle school students do not use effective strategies. To get beyond the literal level, students will have to engage a type of reading that will foster deeper thought and analysis. In other words, they will need to attain academic literacy.

To understand the interactive role of literacy across disciplines, it is important to paint a picture of literacy at the secondary level. According to a joint publication by the Northwest Regional Laboratory, National Council of Teachers of English, and the International Reading Association, levels of literacy can be described as (but not limited to):

Basic Literacy—refers to the ability to decode, recognize, and comprehend printed signs, symbols, and words.
Proficient Literacy—refers to the ability to extend ideas, make inferences, draw conclusions, and make connections to personal experiences from printed texts.
Advanced Literacy—refers to the ability to use language to solve problems and to extend cognitive development. New understandings within and across texts and the ability to summarize, evaluate, and apply strategies to text and construct meaning from various perspectives also describe someone at an advanced level of literacy.

While these levels appear to be clear demarcations of ability, it is feasible that students could move between the various levels depending on prior knowledge of topics, language ability, and other variables that render the lines a little shaggy. A reader who may be at an advanced level could conceivably be faced with text that he or she can decode but not comprehend. In short, the academic literacy demands placed on students require functioning at all three levels. Students who have not acquired agility with academic literacy need concrete examples and continuous support to "mentally map" ways of meeting these demands. What some students lack is the insight that successful readers use when they shift approaches from narrative to expository or subject area text.

Here is an example of the type of reading demanded by one state's sixth-grade history-social studies content standards: "Students analyze the causes and effects of the vast expansion and ultimate disintegration of the Roman Empire." Within this standard, students are also asked to study the strengths and contributions of Rome, including Roman law, architecture, engineering, philosophy, and geographic borders, as well as learn about the Byzantine Empire and Constantinople. Subsequent to this content standard, students explore Mesopotamia, Ancient Egypt, Ancient Greece, and the Hebrews (California Department of Education, 1999). In order to meet the demands of these standards, students will have to do a fair amount of reading, but not a recreational kind of reading.

For middle school teachers and students, the important factors for content-based academic literacy include the following:
- Knowing what to do when they encounter unusual or irregular words that make up so much content-specific vocabulary
- Understanding the organization of the text, which helps set the purpose for reading (that is, cause and effect, problem and solution, sequence, and so forth)
- Maintaining an inventory of effective strategies, including ways of prereading, close reading, re-inspecting, summarizing, and reflecting or reviewing

Today, the role of content-area teachers is to "encourage the thinking processes essential to understanding, i.e., to facilitate learning with text" (Readance, 2000). Teachers who see themselves as facilitators of learning will "apprentice" students to a variety of strategies based upon students' understanding of the organization of text, a purpose for reading the text, and a variety of strategies to engage them in the reading of text. Inherent in this call is the necessity for all teachers to understand that literacy extends to all subject areas.

To become more successful in facilitating content instruction though academic literacy, teachers will need to approach their content though a process focus. Cognitive strategies serve as subtext to the curriculum. Content teachers may be "content rich, but process poor." In other words, they are well versed in the content, but they might not have a command of strategies needed to enhance students' comprehension of text. To become "process rich," teachers will need to have "topical knowledge," an inventory of different reading strategies, and knowledge of when to use a particular strategy. Teachers will also need to explore ways of sharing strategies among the disciplines.

The missing ingredient in middle school literacy efforts has been the lack of continuity across the disciplines. Rather than allowing strategies to remain covert and internal, content teachers will need to externalize and guide students in a way that embeds in academic literacy into a school-wide curriculum. The *Reader's Handbook* allows teachers to do that. The *Reader's Handbook* becomes a vehicle for sharing an inventory of strategies across the entire middle school. Not only do the teachers become "process rich," but the students also begin to understand that there are different types of reading strategies that have distinct uses and some that cross over disciplines.

Through this overt approach to "unpacking" text, students will have topical knowledge of the strategies and also conditional knowledge, in which they know when to use a particular strategy depending on the text they are reading. Through effective teacher modeling with the *Reader's Handbook*, students will improve their ability to shift approaches to reading various forms of text. Students will become more effective learners, and teachers will bring a new dimension to their instructional practice that will allow access to the curriculum for all students.

REFERENCES

Braunger, J. & Lewis, J. (1998). *Building a knowledge base in reading*. Portland: Northwest Regional Education Laboratory.

California Department of Education. (1999). *Reading/language arts framework for California public schools*. Sacramento: CDE Press.

Campbell, J., et al. (1998). *NAEP 1998 Reading Report Card for the Nation and the States*. Washington, D.C.: U.S. Department of Education.

Irvin, J. (1998). *Reading and the middle school student: strategies to enhance literacy*. Boston: Allyn & Bacon.

Readance, J., Bean, T., & Baldwin, S. (2000). *Content area literacy: an integrated approach*. Dubuque: Kendall Hunt.

Creating a Middle School Reading Initiative

by Dennis Jackson and Richard P. Santeusanio

Our goal in writing this article is to identify the seven building blocks required to implement a successful middle school reading initiative. We begin by sharing three fictitious—but common—scenarios that illustrate how some educators with good intentions and good ideas fail to make a difference in a middle school reading program.

The Top Down Approach

Superintendent Dr. Ralph Sullivan of the Top Down City School District doesn't like what he sees as he reviews his middle school's state assessment scores. "Things are going to change around here," he says to himself. "Our kids deserve better than what we are providing for them." So Dr. Sullivan, in his opening day remarks to his staff in the fall, declares that one of the district goals is to improve reading scores, with particular emphasis on the middle school. At the end of the year, the scores from the middle school arrive. There is no improvement. Why?

While it can be argued that it takes more than a year to improve test scores, Dr. Sullivan himself contributed to the stagnant scores because he merely announced reading at the middle school was a priority. He had what Fullan (1999) calls "moral purpose"; he wanted to do what was right for the middle school in his district. But he had no plan to develop a comprehensive middle school program.

The Autonomous Approach

Seventh-grade teacher Marsha Jones at the Independence School wants her students to be good readers, and she knows what to do. "It is time for me to put my master's in reading to work," she tells a friend over a Saturday afternoon lunch.

Marsha does indeed do the job. When the scores for her language arts classes are reported at the end of the school year, significant progress is documented. Her students move on to grade eight to a team of teachers who do not have the same focus on reading Marsha had with her students. The gains made at the end of seventh grade are lost at the end of grade 8. Why?

The simple answer is that while most schools can point to pockets of success and innovation, real and permanent school improvement occurs when teachers work collaboratively and "buy in" to a school-wide reading initiative.

The Commodity Approach

Principal Wayne Mackin of the Materials Middle School wants his students to be the best readers in the state. "We're above average now," he tells his assistant principal, "and we're going to get to the top. We can do it if we can just get the right materials in the hands of our teachers and students."

Wayne does indeed get many new, attractive language arts books into the Materials Middle School classrooms. Teachers and students use the new materials for a few years. And, while the student reading scores continue to be above average, they are far from being among the best in the state. Why?

Principal Mackin did the right thing in providing his teachers and students with resources. But he did not provide the teachers with the training needed to use the materials effectively.

These three scenarios illustrate five of the seven building blocks required to initiate a comprehensive middle school reading program. All seven are needed to implement and sustain an effective reading program.

1. Moral Purpose Fullan (1999) defines moral purpose as ". . . making a positive difference in the lives of all citizens"—in this case, students. However, he also notes that achieving this positive difference is enormously complex, but not impossible. When good things happen in schools, it always starts with someone or a group of educators approaching an issue with a moral purpose.

2. Planning the Change The person or group who plans the middle school reading initiative should consider Fullan's (1991) recommendations in planning the change. As they relate to planning a middle school reading initiative, planners should recognize several things:

- Initial ideas of what the change should be will transform and continue to develop.
- Teachers, the implementers, need to work out their own meaning of what the reading initiative will look like.
- Conflict and disagreement are fundamental to successful change.
- Relearning is at the heart of a change in a middle school reading program.
- Effective change takes time.
- Slow implementation does not mean outright rejection of the values inherent in the reading initiative.
- Not everyone will embrace the reading initiative.
- No amount of technical support and expertise will make it totally clear what action needs to take place to implement the reading initiative.
- The real agenda is changing the culture of the school.

3. Collaboration and "Buy In" Michael Fullan eloquently describes the meaning of a collaborative culture:
"Collaborative organizations fan the passion and emotions of its members because they so value commitment and the energy required to pursue complex goals. But instead of leaving passionate teachers to sink or swim, the true value of collaborative cultures is that they simultaneously encourage passion and provide emotional support as people work through the roller coaster of change" (Fullan, 1999, p. 38).

So what are the characteristics of a collaborative culture? According to Fullan, such cultures foster diversity while building trust, accept the presence of anxiety, create knowledge, combine connectedness with openhandedness, and fuse the spiritual, political, and intellectual.

It is in this kind of a culture that teachers will ultimately "buy in" to something like a middle school reading initiative. This will happen when the vast majority of the staff:

- believes the reading initiative addresses a need.
- is clear about what its role is in implementing the initiative.
- knows how the initiative affects their time, energy, and need for professional development.
- recognizes that the reading initiative will be rewarding in terms of interaction with peers and others (Fullan, 1991).

4. Resources In order for any reading initiative to be successful, the necessary resources must support it. Among the key resources for a successful secondary reading program are materials and time.

• Materials Simply stated, a classroom cannot have too many reading materials. To grow as readers and to learn the content of a discipline, students need the opportunity to explore and read a wide range of texts. These can include novels and nonfiction books, magazines and newspapers, and short stories, poetry, and essays. Make sure that the materials are in as good shape as possible. The subtle message that we give students when we offer them materials that are not well cared for is that we have little respect for the materials (or the students) and that they, in turn, need not show any respect for the materials (or us) (Burke, 2000).

Many schools and districts also provide students with locally developed language arts "guidebooks" that provide students with the tools they need to become stronger readers and more efficient learners. These guidebooks not only define basic standards for the types of activities in which students will engage, but also provide them with guidelines and strategies to help them solve learning and reading challenges they may encounter. They also provide content teachers with a tool for explaining and discussing the learning strategies of their discipline.

• Time The resource of time needs to be considered within the context of both implementing a reading initiative and supporting students as they become more successful readers and learners. Little can be accomplished without the necessary time. In the classroom, students must have the opportunity to both read and discuss their reading—its content and the processes they used to help themselves learn and understand. And initiatives aimed at supporting students' growth as readers and learners need time to develop and grow. In this era of quick fixes, the time to create, implement, reflect upon, and revise an initiative is becoming too rare while, at the same time, increasingly necessary (Braunger and Lewis, 1998).

5. Professional Development (PD) Lyons and Pinnell (2001) provide us with some characteristics to keep in mind when planning and developing PD for a middle school reading initiative. They suggest gathering information about the school; planning a wide variety of learning experiences; establishing clear goals and a common vision; assessing and focusing resources such as time, people, and materials; teaching specific instructional procedures; establishing a culture that encourages reflection, feedback, support, and problem solving; coaching and providing in-class demonstrations; using student data to inform the PD; monitoring the impact of PD; and designing ongoing opportunities.

While the typical PD involves a consultant or university presenter who works with teachers, Robb (2000a) suggests, among a number of PD alternatives, teacher study groups led by a facilitator. For a middle school initiative, for example, math teachers might form a group to discover ways of helping students read word problems and symbols, social studies teachers might focus on maps, charts, and graphs, and language arts teachers might study the reading-writing connection.

6. Key Components of a Comprehensive Reading Program The key components of a comprehensive reading program can be distilled into three simple elements: opportunity, choice, and instruction. Each of these elements applies to all students: our best readers, average readers, and students in need of special intervention.

• **Opportunity** Students (and all members of the school community) need the chance to read often and widely. Initiatives that support this opportunity are independent reading, reading aloud, and programs that provide students with the time to read, such as Sustained Silent Reading (Robb, 2000b).

• **Choice** Allowing students to have a voice in selecting the materials they read ensures that they will be engaged in their reading and that they will read texts that are comprehensible. It is easy to see how choice links directly with the resource of "materials" identified above, since a range of materials provides students with options and relieves teachers of the burden of assigning texts that may be too simple or too challenging for students (Burke, 1999).

• **Instruction** Good teaching supports the role of schools in helping students grow to become literate adults. It is through instruction that we "show them how to do it better." Instruction is the opportunity for schools and teachers to share with students the processes for getting meaning from text as well as the understanding that reading is a problem-solving activity—one that constantly poses challenges to the reader and requires a variety of strategies (Langer, 2000).

7. Sustaining the Effort In these days of high-stakes testing, one of the greatest challenges facing teachers and schools that recognize the importance of establishing a school-wide reading initiative is to support and maintain the effort long enough for it to have an effect on the school and its culture. Too often, we find ourselves forced to take on the short-range focus of a discipline's content rather than the long-range view of developing the processes that make students independent learners of a discipline. One simple strategy for ensuring that any initiative is sustained and supported over time is the use of long- and short-term planning processes.

In the processes, the faculty establishes a year-long goal. It then identifies a step that all staff members can take over the next 30 days. Members work individually or in teams to accomplish the step agreed upon. One month later the staff meets to discuss the outcome of the small step it took: what worked and what did not. Informed by this discussion, the faculty then identifies a second step toward the long-term goal that it will take for the next 30 days. The process of action, reflection, and planning continues throughout the school year, culminating in an evaluation of how well the long-term goal was achieved and the establishment of a new long-term goal for the next school year.

An Example

Let's take a look at how this model might play out using the *Reader's Handbook*. Westside Middle School has declared that improving student learning and reading abilities are its focuses for the school year, and it is committed to using the *Reader's Handbook* as a key tool. At the initial staff meetings for the school year, the staff works to turn this declaration into a plan of action by identifying two long-term goals that it will work to achieve during the school year:

1. to establish a school-wide common language for students and staff to use when talking about how to learn from and understand text.
2. to provide students with the tools to be successful learners in each of their courses.

These two goals are fairly comprehensive, and experience has shown us that working to achieve goals that are too broad can often doom them to failure. So, the staff of Westside, while keeping its long-term goals in mind, establishes a more achievable objective that will move it toward accomplishing the broader goal. After discussion, the Westside faculty determined that during the first half of the school year it would focus only on the first goal: establishing a school-wide common language.

At its initial meeting of the year, the staff worked to achieve the first short-term goal for the year: introduce the *Reader's Handbook* to all students by presenting the opening section, "How to Use This Book." Grade-level teams of math, science, social studies, and language arts teachers planned the specifics of how, over the next 30 days, they would accomplish this short-term goal and shared their plans with the entire staff. During the next month, the teams worked to implement their plan.

At the October staff meeting, each team reported its progress. Successes were shared, and problems were presented. The full group discussed the successes and shared potential solutions to the problems. Then, within the context of both the previous month's accomplishments and the long-term goal of establishing a common language, a new short-term goal for the entire school was established: to introduce the reading process to all students using Chapter 2 of the *Reader's Handbook*.

Again, teams met to devise their plans. Those plans were shared with the full staff and, over the next 30 days, implemented. At the next staff meeting, successes and problems were discussed, and within the context of the long-term goal, a short-term goal for the next 30 days was established.

This process of short-term planning within the context of progress toward long-term goals continued throughout the school year and provided the entire school with the focus and direction that resulted in the successful achievement of its goals. This process has several benefits:

- It provides an opportunity for all members of the school community to contribute to establishing both long- and short-term goals.

- It allows for both successes and issues to be raised and discussed in the process of reflecting and planning. (Too often we only hear about the positives when, in fact, helping to solve the negatives can be the key to a successful initiative.)

- It keeps the initiative up front, as a critical part of the community's discussion and fabric at each monthly meeting.

It is through the use of this or other "stay the course" efforts that the success of any initiative can be assured.

REFERENCES

Braunger, J. & Lewis, J. (1998). *Building a knowledge base in reading.* Portland: Northwest Regional Education Laboratory.

Burke, J. (1999). *The English teacher's companion.* Portsmouth: Boynton/Cook Heinemann.

Burke, J. (2000). *Reading reminders: tools, tips, and techniques.* Portsmouth: Boynton/Cook Heinemann.

Fullan, M. (1991). *The new meaning of education change.* New York: Teachers College Press.

Fullan, M. (1999). *Change forces: the sequel.* New York: Routledge/Falmer Press.

Langer, J. (2000). *Guidelines for teaching middle and high school students to read and write well.* Albany: Center on English Learning & Achievement.

Lyons, C. A & Pinnell, G.S. (2001). *Systems for change in literacy education: a guide to professional development.* Portsmouth: Heinemann.

Robb, L. (2000a). *Redefining staff development.* Portsmouth: Heinemann.

Robb, L. (2000b). *Teaching reading in middle school.* New York: Scholastic.

WEEK 1

Introduction

For use with *Reader's Handbook* pages 24–29

Daily Lessons	Summary*
Lesson 1 **Goals of the Handbook**	Discuss as a class the goals of the *Reader's Handbook*.
Lesson 2 **Uses of the Handbook**	Work with students to explore the *Reader's Handbook* and how it is organized.
Lesson 3 **What Is Reading?**	Create a class definition of reading. Compare it to the definition in the handbook. Help students create a sketch of what they "see" when they read.
Lesson 4 **The Reading and** **Writing Connection**	Review the writing process. Discuss with students the similarities and differences between the reading and writing processes.

*Use these notes to help you teach a mini-lesson or to teach a briefer, shorter version of the lessons for more proficient students.

Lesson Resources

See *Student Applications Book 6* pages 6–7.

See *Teacher's Guide* pages 30–32.

See Website www.greatsource.com/rehand/

For more practice, see also
Daybook Grade 6, pages 20–21.

WEEK 2

The Reading Process
For use with *Reader's Handbook* pages 32–37

Daily Lessons	Summary*
Lesson 1 **The Reading Process**	Work with students to explore the reading process and what it is like for them.
Lesson 2 **Before Reading**	Discuss the first stage in the reading process and why setting a purpose, previewing, and planning are important steps in it.
Lesson 3 **During Reading**	Explore the steps of reading with a purpose and connecting that are involved in this second stage of the reading process.
Lesson 4 **After Reading**	Walk through the last stage of the reading process and explain the importance of reflecting, rereading, and remembering.

*Use these notes to help you teach a mini-lesson or to teach a briefer, shorter version of the lessons for more proficient students.

Lesson Resources

Overheads
For this lesson, use:
Overhead 1: Reading Process

See *Student Applications Book* 6 pages 8–9.

See *Teacher's Guide* pages 34–38.

See Website www.greatsource.com/rehand/

For more practice, see also *Sourcebook* Grade 6, pages 14–15, 12–21; *Daybook* Grade 6, pages 22–23, 26–31.

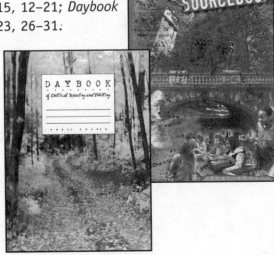

WEEK 1
Lesson 1 ▶ Goals of the Handbook

For use with *Reader's Handbook* pages 14–15

Goals

In this introductory lesson, students learn three main goals of the handbook.

Teaching Focus

Background
Explain the importance of learning what you need to learn. Goals give a journey, a place to point toward. By understanding the goals of the handbook, students will find their learning becomes easier.

Instruction
Help students to understand the importance of having good models, good strategies, and a wide understanding of different kinds of readings. Use an analogy to something in the students' world, like modeling how to bat and field in baseball. Students see how to do something when they see it modeled. Then, they need to learn technique—a way to coil, bend at the knees, hold the bat, and so on. Last, they need to understand the nuances of how to handle different kinds of pitches as a batter. Explain to students that they learn to read the same way.

Either in small groups or as a whole class, discuss with students ways they have learned how to do something and the ways that worked best for them.

Teaching Approach

Use of the Handbook
Ask student volunteers to read through the Goals on pages 14–15. Then discuss which of the goals seems most important to them, and discuss the reasons why. Help students see that all of the goals are important.

Extend the Handbook
Introduce the idea of the handbook goals to the whole class. Then ask students to work in pairs to explore what modeling, learning strategies, and learning about kinds of readings mean. Let students explain to each other why modeling good reading habits will be important and what they mean by using "reading strategies."

Assessment
Ask students:

■ What are you supposed to learn from the *Reader's Handbook*?

■ Why is having a model of how to do something important?

■ When have you used models in other things you do?

■ What kinds of reading strategies do you now use? Do you know enough of them?

■ What sorts of materials do you read, and do you feel prepared to read all of them?

WEEK 1
Lesson 2 — Uses of the Handbook

For use with *Reader's Handbook* pages 16–21

Goals

In this lesson, students explore the *Reader's Handbook* and how it is organized.

Teaching Focus

Background

Before delving into the handbook, students need to take the time to preview it, just as they would other nonfiction texts. Discerning the handbook's organization will give the text a level of predictability and provide a framework for reading.

Instruction

Ask student volunteers to demonstrate what they do before reading a new book. Do they check out the table of contents? Skim through a chapter? Explain that previewing helps readers set a purpose for reading and gain a sense of how the book is organized. Point out that previewing the *Reader's Handbook* will help students understand what it is all about. Look also at the introductory activities in the front of the *Teacher's Guide*. These activities will help students explore different parts of the *Reader's Handbook*.

Teaching Approach

Use of the Handbook

Read aloud and discuss the four uses of the handbook on page 16. Then have students work in small groups to examine the organization of the handbook. Ask them to begin by reviewing the samples on pages 17–21. Have students look through the book for additional examples of its various components.

Extend the Handbook

Encourage groups to continue previewing the handbook by examining the table of contents and any other features that pique their curiosity.

Assessment

Ask students:

■ How might you use the handbook?

■ What did you learn about the handbook by previewing it?

■ How will this lesson help you use the handbook?

WEEK 1
Lesson 3 What Is Reading?

For use with *Reader's Handbook* pages 24–27

Goals

In this lesson, students learn what reading is, why we read, and what happens when we read.

Teaching Focus

Background

A basic understanding of what reading is, why we read, and what happens when we read will enable students to reflect on their own reading experiences and practices. Metacognition—the ability to "think about thinking"—is a critical skill for becoming a more proficient reader. This lesson offers students the opportunity to think metacognitively about reading.

Instruction

With the class, brainstorm ideas about what reading is. Use the brainstorming session to come up with a class definition for reading. Compare it to the definitions on page 24 of the handbook. Use the same process to explore with students the reasons why people read. Then ask student volunteers to describe what they "see" in their minds as they read.

Teaching Approach

Use of the Handbook

Review pages 24–25 of the handbook. Then, have students read pages 26–27. To help students visualize the reading process, invite them to follow the steps on page 27 to create a sketch of how they see themselves as they read.

Extend the Handbook

Have students reflect on their sketches. What do the sketches tell them about how they see reading? Have students work in small groups to share their sketches. How do they relate to the class definition of *reading*?

Assessment

Ask students:

■ Why do you read?

■ Has your definition of *reading* changed after reading this section of the handbook?

■ How will you use this lesson to help you become a better reader?

WEEK 1
Lesson 4 The Reading and Writing Connection

For use with *Reader's Handbook* pages 28–29

Goals

In this lesson, students review the writing process and compare it to the process of reading.

Teaching Focus

Background

While most sixth-graders are probably familiar with the writing process, they may be less familiar with the concept of a "reading process." Reviewing the steps in the writing process and connecting it to the reading process provide a link for students unaccustomed to viewing reading as an active process.

Instruction

Review with students the steps involved in the writing process. Explain that reading is a process, just as writing is. Discuss the similarities and differences between the two activities. You might create a Venn Diagram to illustrate the comparisons. (For more information on Venn Diagrams, see page 683 of the *Reader's Handbook*.)

Teaching Approach

Use of the Handbook

Have students read page 28 of the handbook. Discuss the list of questions. Encourage students to add to the list. Then have students read page 29. Discuss these questions as well, and add others. Return to the Venn Diagram started above. Work with students to modify the diagram based on their reading.

Extend the Handbook

Have students work in small groups to discuss what they learned about reading in this unit. Invite groups to summarize their discussions and share them with the rest of the class.

Assessment

Ask students:

■ How is the reading process similar to the writing process? How is it different?

■ What questions do you still have about reading? How might you get answers?

■ What do you think are the steps in the reading process?

WEEK 2
Lesson 1 The Reading Process

For use with *Reader's Handbook* pages 32–37

Goals

In this lesson, students learn what the reading process is and why it is important.

Teaching Focus

Background

Understanding the significance of the reading process and using it as they read are key to students' reading development. This lesson provides an overview of the process.

Instruction

Invite student volunteers to provide definitions of the term *process*. Work with students to come up with a definition similar to the following: a set of actions performed in a special order that leads to a particular result. Then have students list processes they use everyday, such as making their breakfast or brushing their teeth. Explain that reading is also a process. There are specific steps good readers follow to get the most out of their reading. Introduce the three main stages in the reading process: Before Reading, During Reading, and After Reading.

Teaching Approach

Use of the Handbook

Ask students to skim pages 32–36 to get a sense of what this unit will cover. Then divide the class into three groups. Assign each group one stage of the reading process. Have each group read and summarize their section for the rest of the class.

Extend the Handbook

Either in their journals or orally, have students reflect on which steps of the reading process they already follow and which ones are new to them. Explain that in the lessons to follow they will learn about the three main stages in greater detail.

Assessment

Ask students:

- Why is the reading process important?

- What are the three main stages in the reading process?

- What steps in the reading process do you use now? What steps could you add to help you get the most out of your reading?

WEEK 2
Lesson 2 — Before Reading

For use with *Reader's Handbook* pages 32–33

Goals

In this lesson, students learn about the first stage in the reading process and why it is important to set a purpose, preview, and plan before reading.

Teaching Focus

Background

All too often, students jump right into their reading without taking the time to think about what they are about to read and, more importantly, why they are going to read it. This lesson encourages students to take the time necessary *before* reading so that they will get more out of their reading.

Instruction

Ask students what they do before they read. Perhaps they find a comfortable chair to sit in or turn on a lamp. Explain that there are other steps they should follow before they begin reading. These steps involve *setting a purpose*, *previewing*, and *planning*. Point out that following these steps will not take very much time and will enable them to get more out of their reading.

Teaching Approach

Use of the Handbook

Have students read pages 32–33 of the handbook. Discuss with students what steps they already follow before reading and what steps they need to start using.

Extend the Handbook

Have students take out a blank piece of paper and fold it into thirds. Ask them to use the top third of the paper to list the three steps they should follow before reading. Invite them to make their list colorful and eye-catching. Then have students put an asterisk next to the steps they need to use more. Encourage them to refer to their lists before reading until they have the steps memorized. Explain that they will finish listing the steps in the reading process as they complete the unit.

Assessment

Ask students:

■ What are the three steps to follow before reading?

■ What are the purposes of each step?

■ How will you use this lesson to help you become a better reader?

WEEK 2
Lesson 3 During Reading

For use with *Reader's Handbook* pages 34–35

Goals

In this lesson, students learn about the second stage in the reading process and why it is important to read with a purpose and connect to their reading.

Teaching Focus

Background

Students sometimes think of reading as simply the act of passing their eyes over the words on a page. Good readers know, however, that the act of reading involves much more than this. Focusing on their purpose for reading and connecting what they read to their own lives will enable students to better understand what they read.

Instruction

Ask student volunteers to define reading. What is reading? What do we do as we read? Help students understand that reading is more than the physical act of looking at words on a page. Explain that readers are thinkers, and strong readers know how to focus their thinking on what they want to get out of the reading. They also find ways to connect what they read to their own lives.

Teaching Approach

Use of the Handbook

Read aloud the first paragraph under "Read with a Purpose" on page 34. Articulate to students what you were thinking as you read. For instance, you might say, "What is my purpose for reading? How does my purpose relate to what I'm reading here?"

Ask student volunteers to continue reading page 34 in this fashion. Invite them to first state their purpose. After reading, ask them to articulate what they were thinking as they read and how their thoughts related to their purpose. Then have students read the top half of page 35 on their own. Invite them to write down their purpose before reading. As they read, have them jot down ideas that relate to their purpose or connections they make to the text.

Extend the Handbook

Have students continue their reading process checklists begun in the previous lesson. Ask them to add the steps involved in the During Reading stage. Remind them to put asterisks next to the steps on which they need to work.

Assessment

Ask students:

- What are the steps involved in the During Reading stage?

- What is the purpose of each step?

WEEK 2
Lesson 4 After Reading

For use with *Reader's Handbook* pages 35–37

Goals

In this lesson, students learn about the final stage in the reading process and why it is important to pause and reflect, reread, and remember.

Teaching Focus

Background

Students need to recognize that the reading process doesn't stop once they finish reading. In order to retain information and assimilate what they've read into their lives, strong readers continue the process by reflecting on what they've read, rereading if needed, and devising a plan for remembering what they learned.

Instruction

Invite student volunteers to discuss what they do after reading. Do they close the book and immediately move on to another activity? Or do they pause for a time and think about what they read? Point out to students that in order to remember and understand what they read, it is important to take time once they finish reading to reflect on what they learned.

Teaching Approach

Use of the Handbook

Have students read pages 35–37. Discuss with students what steps they already follow after reading and what steps they need to start incorporating into their reading process.

Extend the Handbook

Have students finish their reading process checklists. Remind them to continue placing asterisks next to the steps they need to remember to use. Students should check the accuracy of their lists against the one shown on page 37. Invite students to refer to their completed checklists as they read to help them remember the steps in the reading process.

Assessment

Ask students:

■ What are the steps to follow after reading?

■ What are the purposes of each step?

■ How will you use this lesson to help you become a better reader?

WEEK 3

Essential Reading Skills For use with *Reader's Handbook* pages 40–42

Daily Lessons	Summary*
Lesson 1 **The Essentials**	Build an understanding of essential reading skills, and explore why these skills are an important part of the reading process.
Lesson 2 **Infer and Conclude**	Discuss as a class the techniques of making inferences and drawing conclusions.
Lesson 3 **Compare and Contrast**	Use a Venn Diagram to discuss the skills of comparing and contrasting.
Lesson 4 **Evaluate**	Work with the class to develop a list of questions students can use to help them evaluate their reading material.

*Use these notes to help you teach a mini-lesson or to teach a briefer, shorter version of the lessons for more proficient students.

Lesson Resources

See *Student Applications Book 6* pages 10–12.

See *Teacher's Guide* pages 40–41.

See Website www.greatsource.com/rehand/

For more practice, see also *Sourcebook* Grade 6, pages 22–30, 50–57; *Daybook* Grade 6 pages 26–31.

54

WEEK 4

Reading Actively

For use with *Reader's Handbook* pages 43–46

Daily Lessons	Summary*
Lesson 1 **Become an Active Reader**	Work with students to define active reading and to list ways students can be active participants in the reading process.
Lesson 2 **Mark Up the Text**	Introduce students to the concept of marking up the text in order to become more active readers.
Lesson 3 **Make the Connection**	Discuss ways of connecting to the text and why some texts are easier to connect to than others.
Lesson 4 **Other Ways to Read Actively**	Examine additional ways of reading actively, including asking questions, visualizing, predicting, and clarifying.

*Use these notes to help you teach a mini-lesson or to teach a briefer, shorter version of the lessons for more proficient students.

Lesson Resources

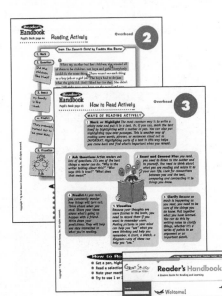

Overheads

For this lesson, use:
Overhead 2: Reading Actively
Overhead 3: How to Read Actively

See *Student Applications Book 6* pages 13–14.

See *Teacher's Guide* pages 42–43.

See Website www.greatsource.com/rehand/

For more practice, see also *Sourcebook* Grade 6, pages 8–10; *Daybook* Grade 6, pages 10–12.

WEEK 3
Lesson 1 The Essentials

For use with *Reader's Handbook* pages 40–42

Goals

In this introductory lesson, students learn what essential reading skills are and why they are an important part of the reading process.

Teaching Focus

Background

The four reading skills discussed in this lesson—making inferences, drawing conclusions, comparing and contrasting, and evaluating—can be viewed as stepping stones to active, critical reading. Mastering these essentials is the first step to becoming a strong reader.

Instruction

Discuss with students the term *essential skills*. Be sure students understand the meaning of the word *essential*. Ask student volunteers to list the essential skills needed for an everyday activity, such as riding a bike. Point out that reading involves some essential skills as well. Explain that this unit will focus on four of the essential skills of reading.

Teaching Approach

Use of the Handbook

Ask students to skim through the section of the handbook that focuses on essential reading skills (pages 40–42). Prior to skimming, you may want to have the whole class discuss their thoughts about what this section will include.

Extend the Handbook

Have students work in pairs to read a paragraph from another text. After reading, ask pairs to discuss what skills they used to read and understand the paragraph. Have partners share the skills they used with the rest of the class. Encourage students to compare these reading skills with those they learn as they continue this unit.

Assessment

Ask students:

■ What does the term *essential skills* mean?

■ What are at least two essential skills of reading?

■ How will you use this lesson to improve your reading "know-how"?

WEEK 3
Lesson 2 — Infer and Conclude

For use with *Reader's Handbook* pages 40–41

Goals

In this lesson, students learn how making inferences and drawing conclusions can help them become better readers.

Teaching Focus

Background

Readers constantly need to make inferences and draw conclusions in order to get the most out of what they read. Although making inferences and drawing conclusions are similar, there are subtle distinctions between the two skills. Both involve connecting the stated (what's on the pages) to the unstated (what we can construe from the stated). Making inferences can be thought of as "reading between the lines." Drawing conclusions involves looking at the information the author provides and deciding what you—the reader—think it means.

Instruction

Explain to students that an inference or conclusion is a connection made between what is known and what is unknown. People make inferences and draw conclusions all the time. For example, what would students infer from smelling smoke? What conclusions could they draw from hearing a siren? Discuss with students other examples of making inferences and drawing conclusions. Explain that readers make inferences and draw conclusions as well.

Teaching Approach

Use of the Handbook

Ask student volunteers to read aloud page 40. Ask students to pay particular attention to the "making inferences" equation. As a class, discuss why making inferences is sometimes called "reading between the lines." Then read page 41. Use the example provided to illustrate how facts can be used to draw conclusions.

Extend the Handbook

Ask students to work with partners to practice making inferences and drawing conclusions. Invite partners to choose another text, either a class novel or a textbook. Have one partner read a paragraph or two aloud. Then encourage partners to state what inferences they made or what conclusions they were able to draw from what they read.

Assessment

Ask students:

■ What does "making inferences" mean?

■ Why is drawing conclusions important when you read?

■ Daily Lesson Plan

WEEK 3
Lesson 3 Compare and Contrast

For use with *Reader's Handbook* page 42

Goals

In this lesson, students learn ways to compare and contrast as they read.

Teaching Focus

Background

Readers are always making comparisons—between two characters, between two authors' styles, between different perspectives. Comparing and contrasting enables us to better understand what we read by connecting our reading to other ideas and often by connecting to things we already know.

Instruction

Draw a Venn Diagram on the board. (See page 683 in the handbook for an example.) Explain to students the different parts of the diagram. Invite a volunteer to suggest two things to compare, such as two fairy tales or two types of sports. Work with students to fill in the Venn Diagram. Ask students what they learned from comparing and contrasting these two things. Explain that readers, too, compare and contrast and that this lesson will teach them ways to do so as they read.

Teaching Approach

Use of the Handbook

Either in small groups or as a whole class, have students read the section on comparing and contrasting on page 42 of the handbook. Pay particular attention to the graphic. Work with students to add more questions to those listed in the graphic. (For example, "How is this character like me? How is he or she different?") Encourage students to include questions for reading nonfiction materials, such as "How is this culture similar to my own? How is it different?"

Extend the Handbook

Have students choose one of the questions they generated above or one listed on the graphic on page 42. Invite students to answer the question using a piece of writing (such as a class novel or textbook) with which they are familiar. Encourage students to use a Venn Diagram to help them compare and contrast.

Assessment
Ask students:

■ What is one question you can ask to help yourself compare and contrast?

■ Why is comparing and contrasting important when reading?

■ How can comparing and contrasting help you get more out of your reading?

58

© GREAT SOURCE. ALL RIGHTS RESERVED.

WEEK 3
Lesson 4 Evaluate

For use with *Reader's Handbook* page 42

Goals

In this lesson, students learn ways to evaluate what they read and why evaluating is an essential reading skill.

Teaching Focus

Background

Good readers know that it is not enough simply to comprehend what they read. They must also make judgments about what they read. Are the characters believable? Does the author support his or her opinion with solid evidence? Are the facts accurate? *Evaluating* what is read is crucial for true understanding and appreciation of the text.

Instruction

Work with students to come up with a definition for *evaluating*. Lead them to recognize that to evaluate is to make a judgment about something or someone. Explain that students give and are given evaluations all the time. Point out that report cards, movie reviews, and CD ratings are all examples of evaluations. Can students think of other examples of evaluating?

Teaching Approach

Use of the Handbook

Read aloud the section on evaluating on page 42 of the handbook. Either in small groups or as a whole class, have students develop a list of questions to help them evaluate what they read. Examples might include: Do I trust this character? Is this information helpful? What facts are missing?

Extend the Handbook

Have students return to whatever reading material they were using in the previous lessons. Ask them to write two questions they could ask to help them evaluate what they read. Students can then answer the questions. Discuss how evaluating improved their understanding or appreciation of the material.

Assessment

Ask students:

■ What does the word *evaluate* mean?

■ How can you evaluate what you read?

■ Why is evaluating an important part of the reading process?

WEEK 4
Lesson 1 Become an Active Reader

For use with *Reader's Handbook* pages 43–46

Goals

In this lesson, students learn what it means to be an active reader.

Teaching Focus

Background

Reading is an active process; it requires constant interaction between reader and text. Meaning is not found simply in the words on the page. Active readers construct meaning based on their interpretations of the words. Students unfamiliar with their role as readers need specific instruction on ways to read actively.

Instruction

Discuss with students what it means to be active. Talk about the differences between an active body and an active mind. Point out the relationship between the words *active* and *activity*. Brainstorm a list of activities students do daily. Explain that just as activities such as exercising and walking your dog are active processes for your body, reading is an active process for your mind.

Teaching Approach

Use of the Handbook

As a whole class, read through pages 43–46 of the handbook. Have students pay particular attention to the model on page 44. On the board, list the different ways of reading actively. Explain that in the lessons to follow students will learn more about each of these techniques.

Extend the Handbook

Have students work in small groups to discuss which active reading techniques they use already and which ones they need to add to their reading repertoire.

For additional practice, use pages 13–14 of the *Student Applications Book 6*.

Assessment

Ask students:

■ What does it mean to "read actively"?

■ How will reading actively help you become a better reader?

WEEK 4
Lesson 2   Mark Up the Text

For use with *Reader's Handbook* pages 43–45

Goals

In this lesson, students learn ways to mark up the text and gain understanding of how marking up the text helps them read actively.

Teaching Focus

Background

Walk into any college classroom and you'll find texts filled with marks: highlighted words and phrases, notes jotted in the margins, question marks by confusing parts. College students recognize that marking up the text is one of the best ways to become involved in their reading. Younger students can benefit from these same techniques.

Instruction

Explain to students that one way to read actively is to mark up the text. Discuss ways to do this, including highlighting important information, putting a question mark next to confusing ideas or unfamiliar words, and noting reactions in the margins. Remind students that if they are reading borrowed texts, they will modify this technique so as not to damage the book. (They might use sticky notes in the margins or highlighting tape over key passages.)

Teaching Approach

Use of the Handbook

Ask students to read page 43 to themselves. Then, as a whole class, review the model on page 44. Ask student volunteers to discuss the examples of marking up the text on this page.

Extend the Handbook

Have students create an active reading plan in their journals. Invite them to begin by listing ways they can mark up the text the next time they read. Encourage them to reflect on how they think these techniques will help them read more actively. What do they hope to gain by marking up the text?

Assessment

Ask students:

■ Why is marking up the text important?

■ What are three ways you can mark up a text?

■ How can this lesson help you keep track of your thinking during reading?

WEEK 4
Lesson 3 ▶ Make the Connection

For use with *Reader's Handbook* pages 43–45

Goals

In this lesson, students learn the importance of connecting to what they read.

Teaching Focus

Background

Reacting and connecting to what they read enables readers to make the material their own. Through making connections to the text, readers activate their prior knowledge and create links between their reading and their own lives.
They also see their reading as more relevant and having more purpose.

Instruction

Explain to students that another way to become an active reader is to connect to what they are reading. Ask students their it means to "connect" to what they read. Help them recognize that one way of connecting to the text involves comparing what they read to something in their own lives. Point out that when readers connect to their reading, they make it their own.

Teaching Approach

Use of the Handbook

Have students reread pages 43–45. Discuss ways they might connect the sample on page 44 to something in their own lives. Talk about challenges involved in trying to make such connections, especially when the connection is not immediately obvious.

Extend the Handbook

Have students choose a new piece of writing. It might be a passage from a textbook, a poem, or a page from a novel they would like to read. Ask students to practice connecting to what they read by jotting down their thoughts and reactions to the piece. Ask student volunteers to discuss their reactions to this activity. Was it easy or difficult to connect to the text? Why?

For more practice, use pages 13–14 in the *Student Applications Book 6*.

Assessment

Ask students:

■ What does it mean to "connect to the text"?

■ What is one way you can connect to the text?

■ How can connecting to the text help you get more out of what you read?

WEEK 4
Lesson 4 Other Ways to Read Actively

For use with *Reader's Handbook* pages 43–45

Goals

In this lesson, students learn additional ways to read actively, including asking questions, visualizing, predicting, and clarifying.

Teaching Focus

Background

Active reading helps keep the reader focused on the text. It also enables the reader to better construct meaning during reading. There are a variety of ways to read actively; not all of them work for every reading situation. Having a repertoire of active reading techniques available to them will help students choose those ways that work best for the specific reading task.

Instruction

Review with students the two techniques of active reading discussed so far in this chapter. Explain that there are many other ways to be an active reader. Brainstorm with students some of these ways. To help them brainstorm, encourage students to use what they remember from their previous reading of this chapter in the handbook.

Teaching Approach

Use of the Handbook

Invite students to work in pairs to review pages 43–45. Have pairs work together to write a summary of the chapter. Ask partners to discuss which active reading techniques they find easy to use and which they have more difficulty understanding. Have students put asterisks next to the more difficult techniques.

Extend the Handbook

Have students remain in their pairs. Ask pairs to choose a piece of writing. (They might choose the same piece they used in the previous lesson.) Using page 44 of the handbook as a guide, have students apply the techniques learned in this unit to read the passage actively.

Assessment

Ask students:

■ What is the most important piece of information you learned from this chapter? Why?

■ What was the most difficult part of this chapter for you? Why?

■ How will you use this chapter to help you become a stronger reader?

WEEK 5

Reading Know-how: Reading Paragraphs

For use with *Reader's Handbook* pages 47–54

Daily Lessons	Summary*
Lesson 1 **The Paragraph**	Review with students the characteristics of a paragraph and preview the upcoming unit.
Lesson 2 **The Subject of a Paragraph**	Work with students to identify ways to determine the subject of a paragraph, and discuss why it is important to know the subject.
Lesson 3 **The Stated Main Idea**	Discuss with students what a main idea is and how to find the stated main idea in a paragraph.
Lesson 4 **The Implied Main Idea**	Help students explore ways to identify the implied main idea of a paragraph.

*Use these notes to help you teach a mini-lesson or to teach a briefer, shorter version of the lessons for more proficient students.

Lesson Resources

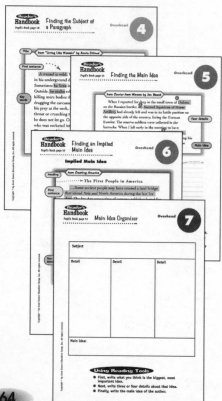

Overheads

For this lesson, use:
Overhead 4: Finding the Subject of a Paragraph
Overhead 5: Finding the Main Idea
Overhead 6: Finding an Implied Main Idea
Overhead 7: Main Idea Organizer

See *Student Applications Book 6* pages 15–18.

See *Teacher's Guide* pages 44–45.

See Website www.greatsource.com/rehand/

For more practice, see also *Sourcebook* Grade 6, pages 12–21; *Daybook* Grade 6, pages 33–34.

WEEK 6

Reading Know-how: Reading Paragraphs
(continued)

For use with *Reader's Handbook* pages 56–63

Daily Lessons	Summary*
Lesson 5 **Paragraph Organization: Time Order**	Discuss as a class the various ways paragraphs can be organized, and take a closer look at time-order organization.
Lesson 6 **Paragraph Organization: Location Order**	Build an understanding of the characteristics of location-order paragraphs.
Lesson 7 **Paragraph Organization: Cause-Effect Order**	Review with the class the cause-effect relationship. Discuss characteristics of paragraphs organized in cause-effect order.
Lesson 8 **Paragraph Organization: Comparison-Contrast Order**	Review with the class what it means to compare and contrast. Have students use a Venn Diagram to help them understand paragraphs organized in comparison-contrast order.

*Use these notes to help you teach a mini-lesson or to teach a briefer, shorter version of the lessons for more proficient students.

Lesson Resources

See *Student Applications Book 6* pages 15–18.

See *Teacher's Guide* pages 46–49.

See Website www.greatsource.com/rehand/

For more practice, see also *Sourcebook* Grade 6, pages 12–21; *Daybook* Grade 6, pages 33–34.

WEEK 5
Lesson 1 The Paragraph

For use with *Reader's Handbook* pages 47–63

Goals

In this introductory lesson, students review what they know about paragraphs and preview this section of the handbook.

Teaching Focus

Background

Paragraphs form the foundation of a vast array of written material. Often, key paragraphs can be viewed as microcosms of the entire text. Understanding the components of a paragraph, and how paragraphs are organized will benefit students not only in their reading but in their writing as well.

Instruction

Discuss with the class what a paragraph is and what elements a paragraph might include. Work with students to create a list of characteristics of paragraphs. Explain to students that understanding paragraphs and their components will help them become stronger readers and writers.

Teaching Approach

Use of the Handbook

Have pairs of students preview pages 47–63 of the handbook. Encourage them to read the headings and subheadings, examine the graphics and illustrations, and examine any other features of this section that interest them. Come together as a whole class and discuss what students learned from previewing the section.

Extend the Handbook

To set a purpose for reading this section of the handbook, have students jot down their thoughts about what they hope to learn as they read. Encourage them to turn their thoughts into personal goals. Have students review their goals as they work through this unit.

For additional practice, see pages 15–18 of the *Student Applications Book 6*.

Assessment

Ask students:

■ What do you know about paragraphs?

■ What do you hope to learn by reading about paragraphs?

■ Why is understanding paragraphs an important part of becoming a strong reader?

WEEK 5
Lesson 2 The Subject of a Paragraph

For use with *Reader's Handbook* pages 48–49

Goals

In this lesson, students discover ways to identify the subject of a paragraph, including looking at the title or heading, the first sentence, and/or key or repeated words.

Teaching Focus

Background
Before readers can determine the main idea of a paragraph, they need to identify who or what the paragraph is about. While students do much of this without even realizing it, they will benefit from step-by-step guidance.

Instruction
Explain to students that in order to understand who or what a paragraph is about, readers must first identify its subject. Point out that there are three main ways to do this:
1. Look at the title or heading.
2. Read the first sentence.
3. Note key or repeated words or names.

Teaching Approach

Use of the Handbook
As a whole class, read page 48. Have students pay particular attention to the sample paragraph. Work with students to identify the various ways they can find the subject of a paragraph. Then have students read page 49 to themselves. Encourage them to refer back to the sample on page 48 as they read each of the three ways to identify the subject.

Extend the Handbook
Have partners examine a paragraph or two from a class textbook. Encourage partners to discuss not only who or what the paragraph's subject is but also what clues they used to identify the subject.

For more practice, see pages 15–18 of the *Student Applications Book 6*.

Assessment
Ask students:

■ Why does it matter who or what the subject of a paragraph is?

■ What are three ways to identify the subject of a paragraph?

WEEK 5
Lesson 3 — The Stated Main Idea

For use with *Reader's Handbook* pages 50–51

Goals

In this lesson, students learn how to determine the stated main idea of a paragraph.

Teaching Focus

Background

Informational texts can bombard readers with hundreds, if not thousands, of words and ideas. Sifting through these words and ideas to determine what the author is really saying about a subject is critical for making sense of and retaining what is read. This lesson begins instruction on main ideas by focusing on the type of main idea easiest to recognize—the stated main idea.

Instruction

Review with students what a main idea is. Point out that the main idea of a piece is the most important thing the author has to say about a subject. Explain that many, but not all, nonfiction paragraphs contain a main idea as well. Determining the main idea of each paragraph will help to determine the main idea of the whole piece. Explain that there are two types of main ideas, stated and implied, and that this lesson will focus on the stated main idea.

Teaching Approach

Use of the Handbook

Divide the class into two groups. Have one group read and discuss page 50; have the second group read and discuss page 51. Ask each group to "teach" their section to the class.

Extend the Handbook

One of the best ways to practice identifying a stated main idea is to write paragraphs containing stated main ideas. Provide students with a broad topic, such as their favorite season or their silliest moment. For an extra challenge, invite students to write two paragraphs on the same topic—one with the main idea in the first sentence and one with the main idea in the last.

Assessment

Ask students:

■ What is a main idea of a paragraph?

■ Why is it important to recognize the main idea?

■ How can identifying the main idea help you make sense out of what you read?

WEEK 5
Lesson 4 — The Implied Main Idea

For use with *Reader's Handbook* pages 52–54

Goals

In this lesson, students learn ways of identifying the implied main idea of a paragraph.

Teaching Focus

Background

Stated main ideas are relatively simple to uncover; they are right there on the page. But in most paragraphs, especially those in more sophisticated texts, the main idea is not always obvious. Readers must *infer* what the main idea is from what is right there on the page. This is a much more complex skill, and a review of inferencing (see page 40 of the handbook) might be necessary before beginning this lesson.

Instruction

Review with the class what it means to *infer*. Remind students that to infer is to "read between the lines." Explain that in most paragraphs the main idea is not stated in the first or last sentence; it is *implied*. And while finding the implied main idea is a bit trickier than finding the stated main idea, there are clues readers can use to uncover it.

Teaching Approach

Use of the Handbook

As a whole class, read the information on page 52. Work with the students to examine the sample paragraph. Discuss the clues in the paragraph that can help them determine the main idea. Then have students read page 53 by themselves. Come back as a whole class to discuss the Main Idea Organizer on the bottom of page 53.

Extend the Handbook

Have students return to the paragraphs they wrote in the previous lesson. Ask them to rewrite their paragraphs, but this time have them imply the main idea rather than state it directly. Invite students to trade paragraphs with a partner. Can partners identify the implied main ideas in the paragraphs? If not, encourage students to rewrite to make the main idea clearer.

For more practice, see pages 15–18 of the *Student Applications Book 6*.

Assessment

Ask students:

■ What is an implied main idea?

■ How is it different from a stated main idea?

■ How will you use this lesson to become a stronger reader?

WEEK 6
Lesson 5

Paragraph Organization: Time Order

For use with *Reader's Handbook* pages 56–57

Goals

In this lesson, students identify the six different ways paragraphs can be organized. Students then examine time-order organization in more detail.

Teaching Focus

Background

Typically, paragraphs are organized in one of six ways: time order, location order, order of importance, cause-effect order, comparison-contrast order, and classification order. Recognizing the underlying structure of a paragraph makes it easier for the reader to track information.

Instruction

Explain to students that most paragraphs are organized in one of six ways (see above). List the six ways on the board. Invite student volunteers to discuss characteristics you might find in each type of paragraph. List these as well. Tell students that in the lessons that follow, they will be examining in greater detail four of these ways to organize a paragraph, starting with time order. Modify the lists as necessary as students read through this section of the handbook.

Teaching Approach

Use of the Handbook

Read aloud page 56 of the handbook. Then have students read to themselves page 57 to learn more about paragraphs organized by time order. Discuss how the graphic organizer on the bottom of page 57 can be used to keep track of paragraphs that use time order. For more information on Timelines, see page 681 of the handbook.

Extend the Handbook

Invite students to try their hand at writing time-order paragraphs. Topics that work well with this type of structure include steps in a process, descriptions of a typical day, and mini-autobiographies.

Assessment

Ask students:

■ What are the characteristics of time-order organization?

■ What tools can you use to keep track of information in a paragraph organized in time order?

WEEK 6
Lesson 6 Paragraph Organization: Location Order

For use with *Reader's Handbook* page 58

Goals

In this lesson, students examine paragraphs organized in location order.

Teaching Focus

Background

Location order is not used as commonly as some of the other types of paragraph organization. However, location order is an important format to understand, since descriptive paragraphs often use some type of location order as their foundation.

Instruction

Invite students to close their eyes as you read the sample paragraph on page 58 aloud. Ask student volunteers to describe what they "saw" as you read. Explain that this type of paragraph is organized in location order. Point out that location-order paragraphs are often rich in description, lending themselves to detailed visualizations on the reader's part.

Teaching Approach

Use of the Handbook

As a whole class, read the rest of page 58 of the handbook. Review the map of location on the bottom of the page. Does it help students "see" the location better? Discuss their answers.

Extend the Handbook

Invite students to think of a favorite place. It might be their bedrooms or a special park or beach. Have students write a paragraph about their place using location-order organization. When they finish, have students read their paragraphs to a partner. Invite the partner to draw a map of what they "see." Ask partners to discuss how the maps compare with the paragraphs.

For more practice, see pages 15–18 of the *Student Applications Book 6*.

Assessment

Ask students:

■ What are the characteristics of paragraphs organized in location order?

■ Why do you think authors use location-order paragraphs in their writing?

■ Why is it important to determine how a paragraph is organized?

WEEK 6
Lesson 7 # Paragraph Organization: Cause-Effect Order

For use with *Reader's Handbook* page 59

Goals

In this lesson, students examine the cause-effect order of paragraph organization.

Teaching Focus

Background

Paragraphs organized in cause-effect order enable readers to more easily make connections between a result and the events that preceded it. Since understanding cause and effect is crucial to understanding the cause-effect order of paragraphs, you might review with students cause and effect before beginning this lesson. (For more information on cause and effect, see page 275 of the handbook.)

Instruction

Review with the class the relationship between cause and effect. Explain that a *cause* is an event that brings about something else (the *effect*). Ask student volunteers to give examples of cause-effect relationships (for example, not brushing your teeth causes tooth decay or watering a plant causes it to grow). Explain that some paragraphs are organized in cause-effect order.

Teaching Approach

Use of the Handbook

Have students work in pairs to read page 59 of the handbook. Encourage partners to pay close attention to the sample paragraph.

For more practice on cause-effect relationships, have partners create a Cause-Effect Organizer much like the one found on page 667 of the handbook. Use the details in the sample paragraph to fill in the organizer.

Extend the Handbook

Have partners work together to craft a short cause-effect paragraph. Encourage them to first create a Cause-Effect Organizer to help them plan the paragraph.

Assessment

Ask students:

■ What are the characteristics of a paragraph organized in cause-effect order?

■ What tools can you use to better keep track of information in a cause-effect paragraph?

WEEK 6
Lesson 8 Paragraph Organization: Comparison-Contrast Order

For use with *Reader's Handbook* page 62

Goals

In this lesson, students examine paragraphs structured in comparison-contrast order.

Teaching Focus

Background

Comparing and contrasting are reading skills that many students begin to master early on in their reading careers. Their prior knowledge of what it means to compare and contrast will help students more easily grasp this form of paragraph organization. (For students who need more help understanding comparison and contrast, see page 278 of the handbook.)

Instruction

Discuss with the class what it means to compare and contrast. Ask student volunteers to name two things that can be compared. Create a Venn Diagram for the example. Work with students to fill in the diagram with characteristics that illustrate how the two things are alike and how they are different. Explain that writers sometimes use comparison-contrast order to organize paragraphs, especially when they want to highlight the similarities and differences between two or more things.

Teaching Approach

Use of the Handbook

Ask students to read page 62 of the handbook by themselves. Then have them create a Venn Diagram for the sample paragraph. (See page 683 of the handbook for more information on Venn Diagrams.) Discuss how creating a Venn Diagram or writing a list like the one on page 62 helps them keep track of the information in the paragraph.

Extend the Handbook

Have students write short comparison-contrast paragraphs. Students might write about how they and a good friend are alike and different, or they might choose to compare two places or two activities. Ask students to share their paragraphs with a partner. Have partners create Venn Diagrams for each other's paragraphs. Point out that the more details the author provides, the easier it is to fill the Venn Diagram in.

Assessment

Ask students:

■ What are the characteristics of paragraphs organized in comparison-contrast order?

■ What lesson in this unit was the most difficult for you? Why?

WEEK 7

Reading Geography

For use with *Reader's Handbook* pages 84–95

Daily Lessons	Summary*
Lesson 1 **Reading Geography:** **An Overview**	Work with the class to preview this section of the handbook. Help students set their own purposes for reading.
Lesson 2 **Geography:** **Before Reading**	Review with students the Before Reading stage of the reading process. Discuss how to apply it to geography material.
Lesson 3 **Geography:** **During Reading**	Explore various graphic organizers and discuss their use when reading geography.
Lesson 4 **How Geography** **Textbooks Are** **Organized**	Discuss with the class common characteristics of geography textbooks. Examine in detail two features: topic organization and the use of graphics.

*Use these notes to help you teach a mini-lesson or to teach a briefer, shorter version of the lessons for more proficient students.

Lesson Resources

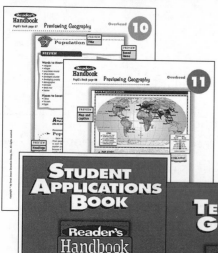

Overheads

For this lesson, use:
Overheads 10 and 11: Previewing Geography

See *Student Applications Book 6* pages 29–38.

See *Teacher's Guide* pages 62–72.

See Website www.greatsource.com/rehand/

See *Content Area Guide: Social Studies.*

For more practice, see also *Sourcebook* Grade 6, pages 84–91; *Daybook* Grade 6, pages 130–134.

Reading Geography (continued)

For use with *Reader's Handbook* pages 96–99

Daily Lessons	Summary*
Lesson 5 **Reading Geography: Connecting to the Text**	Help students make connections between geography materials and their own lives.
Lesson 6 **Geography: After Reading**	Review with the class the After Reading stage of the reading process and how to apply it to reading geography.
Lesson 7 **Rereading Strategy: Note-taking**	Discuss with students how and why to take notes when reading geography.
Lesson 8 **Reading Geography: A Review**	Ask students to use the After Reading activities discussed in Lesson 6 to help them review and remember the information in this section of the *Reader's Handbook*.

*Use these notes to help you teach a mini-lesson or to teach a briefer, shorter version of the lessons for more proficient students.

Lesson Resources

Overheads
For this lesson, use:
Overheads 10 and 11: Previewing Geography

See *Student Applications Book 6* pages 29–38.

See *Teacher's Guide* pages 62–72.

See Website www.greatsource.com/rehand/

See *Content Area Guide: Social Studies.*

For more practice, see also
Sourcebook Grade 6, pages 84–91;
Daybook Grade 6, pages 130–134.

WEEK 7
Lesson 1 — Reading Geography: An Overview

For use with *Reader's Handbook* pages 84–99

Goals

In this introductory lesson, students preview to familiarize themselves with the Reading Geography section of the *Reader's Handbook*.

Teaching Focus

Background

The Reading Geography lesson in the handbook uses the reading process to walk students through a lesson in an actual geography textbook. Previewing the lesson will help students develop prior knowledge about the text and give them something to which they can link their learning.

Instruction

Ask student volunteers to describe what they do when they read a geography textbook. Do they check out the table of contents before reading? Do they flip through the book and look at some of the maps? Review the reading process with the class. Discuss with students how they can use the reading process to help them better understand and remember information in a geography textbook. (For students who need a review of the reading process, see pages 32–37 of the handbook.)

Teaching Approach

Use of the Handbook

Read aloud page 84 of the handbook. Discuss the goals listed on this page. Then have pairs of students preview this section of the handbook. Encourage them to read the headings and subheadings, examine the graphics and illustrations, and explore any other features that interest them. Come together as a whole class and discuss what students learned from previewing the section.

Extend the Handbook

To set their purpose for reading this section of the handbook, have students jot down their thoughts about what they hope to learn as they read. Encourage them to turn their thoughts into personal goals. Have students review their goals as they work through this unit.

Assessment

Ask students:

■ How will using the reading process help you better understand the information in geography textbooks?

■ What did you learn from previewing it?

WEEK 7
Lesson 2 Geography: Before Reading

For use with *Reader's Handbook* pages 85–91

Goals

In this lesson, students review the Before Reading stage of the reading process and learn how and why to apply it to reading geography.

Teaching Focus

Background
As in other content reading areas, setting a purpose, previewing, and planning are crucial activities to use prior to reading geography. These steps will activate prior knowledge and provide a framework for reading to help students stay focused on the material.

Instruction
Ask students to describe what they did before beginning this section in the handbook. Explain that by skimming the section and setting goals for their reading, they were using techniques from the Before Reading stage of the reading process. Discuss how setting a purpose, previewing, and planning helped them get a sense of what this section will be about. Explain that readers can use these same techniques before reading geography.

Teaching Approach

Use of the Handbook
As a whole class, read and discuss page 85 of the handbook. Then read the preview checklist on page 86, and have students work with a partner to preview the geography material on pages 87–90. Discuss as a whole class students' reactions to the previewing process. Finish the discussion by working with the class to plan for reading (page 91).

Extend the Handbook
Have students choose a chapter from a class geography text. Ask them to set a purpose for reading, preview the material, and then make a plan for reading. Invite students to jot down their thoughts about this process in their journals. Questions they might address include these: What did I gain from setting a purpose, previewing, and planning? Which part of the Before Reading process was most difficult for me to do? Why?

Assessment
Ask students:

■ Why should you apply Before Reading strategies to geography material?

■ What are three things to preview?

WEEK 7
Lesson 3 Geography: During Reading

For use with *Reader's Handbook* pages 92–93

Goals

In this lesson, students learn how graphic organizers can help them manage their reading of geography textbooks.

Teaching Focus

Background

Graphic organizers are helpful tools for managing geography information. K-W-L Charts, Concept Maps, and Main Idea Organizers all help students keep track of the facts as they read. For more information on graphic organizers, see pages 666–684 of the *Reader's Handbook*.

Instruction

Review with students the During Reading stage of the reading process. Remind them that one of the most important things to do while reading a geography textbook is to read with a purpose in mind. Discuss how students can use graphic organizers to stay focused on their purposes for reading.

Teaching Approach

Use of the Handbook

Have a student volunteer read the first half of page 92 in the *Reader's Handbook*. Then divide the class into three groups. Ask one group to read about K-W-L Charts, the second group to read about Concept Maps, and the third to read about Main Idea Organizers. Have the groups "teach" their graphic organizer to the rest of the class. Then discuss the purposes of each graphic organizer. When and why would students use each?

Extend the Handbook

Have students return to the geography textbook they previewed in the previous lesson. Ask them to review their purpose and then to read the chapter with their purpose in mind. Have them use a K-W-L Chart, a Concept Map, or a Main Idea Organizer to help them manage their reading.

For more practice, see pages 29–38 in the *Student Applications Book 6*.

Assessment
Ask students:

■ How do graphic organizers help you keep track of geography facts?

■ How will this lesson help you get more out of reading geography?

WEEK 7
Lesson 4
How Geography Textbooks Are Organized

For use with *Reader's Handbook* pages 94–95

Goals

In this lesson, students explore two common features of geography textbook organization.

Teaching Focus

Background

Familiarizing themselves with the structure of a geography text enables readers to better organize their reading of it. A familiar text structure provides a framework on which students can "hang" the important details of their reading.

Instruction

Explain to students that most geography textbooks are organized in similar ways. This helps readers keep track of the information. Work with the class to list common features of a geography textbook. The list might include features such as *headings and subheadings, graphics,* and *boldface geographic terms*. Explain that in this section of the *Reader's Handbook*, students will read about two important features of geography texts: topic organization and the use of graphics.

Teaching Approach

Use of the Handbook

Read aloud the first paragraph on page 94. Then, either as a whole class or in small groups, have students read and discuss the rest of page 94 and page 95. Discuss why summarizing a graphic in one or two sentences is important.

Extend the Handbook

Have students work in pairs to examine the organization of a class geography book. Encourage pairs to focus on one topic and create a topic organization outline similar to the one on page 94 of the handbook. Ask them to pick one or two graphics and write short summaries of them.

For more practice, see pages 29–38 of the *Student Applications Book 6*.

Assessment

Ask students:

■ What are some common features of geography textbooks?

■ Why is it important to understand how a geography textbook is organized?

■ How will you use this lesson to become a stronger reader?

WEEK 8
Lesson 5
Reading Geography: Connecting to the Text

For use with *Reader's Handbook* page 96

Goals

In this lesson, students discover ways to connect geography reading to their own lives.

Teaching Focus

Background

One of the most difficult aspects of the reading process for readers of geography textbooks is making connections between the information presented in the text and their own lives. We can too easily get bogged down in the graphics and statistics and forget that one of our "jobs" during reading is to connect to the text.

Instruction

Review with students the importance of connecting to the text. (For students who need a greater understanding of this aspect of the reading process, see page 35 of the handbook.) Ask students how they might make connections to their geography textbook. Then discuss the differences between trying to make connections to stories and trying to make connections to geography material. Work with students to help them understand that while it might be more difficult to connect to textbooks, it will help them remember (and enjoy) what they read.

Teaching Approach

Use of the Handbook

Read aloud or have a student volunteer read aloud the top of page 96 of the *Reader's Handbook*. Using the class discussion from above and the examples in the text, list ways students can connect to the material. Invite students to brainstorm other examples to add to the list.

Extend the Handbook

Have students return to the geography text they used in previous lessons. Ask them to read a short chapter and then jot down ways they were able to connect to their reading. Was it easy or difficult for students to make connections? Why?

Assessment

Ask students:

■ Why is it important to connect to geography textbooks?

■ What are two ways you can connect to your geography reading?

WEEK 8
Lesson 6 Geography: After Reading

For use with *Reader's Handbook* pages 97 and 99

Goals

In this lesson, students learn how to apply the After Reading stage of the reading process to geography texts.

Teaching Focus

Background
One of the most common reasons for reading geography textbooks is to learn new information. In order to fulfill this purpose, readers need to apply the steps in the After Reading stage of the reading process (pause and reflect, reread, remember) to the material.

Instruction
Review with students the After Reading stage of the reading process. (Have students reread pages 35–36 of the *Reader's Handbook* if necessary.) Discuss the three parts of in this stage.

Teaching Approach

Use of the Handbook
Read aloud the top of page 97. Work with the class to complete the K-W-L Chart from page 92. Then, ask a student volunteer to read the rest of the page. Have students read page 99 to themselves. (Note-taking on page 98 will be discussed in detail in the next lesson.)

Extend the Handbook
Have students return to the chapter of the geography textbook they have been using throughout this unit. Ask them to follow the steps in the After Reading stage to this material. Then, have them come together as a whole class to discuss their work. Which part of the assignment did students find the easiest to do? Which was the most difficult? How did applying these After Reading strategies affect their understanding of the chapter?

For more practice, see pages 29–38 of the *Student Applications Book 6*.

Assessment
Ask students:

■ How can you apply After Reading activities to geography textbooks?

■ What is the most important thing you learned from this lesson? Explain.

WEEK 8
Lesson 7 Rereading Strategy: Note-taking

For use with *Reader's Handbook* page 98

Goals

In this lesson, students learn how and why to take notes when rereading geography textbooks.

Teaching Focus

Background

Note-taking enables readers to organize information in a text. The key, however, is to be able to determine what information to include when using note-taking. Good notes should provide readers with all they need to review and remember from the reading material. For a more detailed discussion of note-taking, see pages 646–647 of the *Reader's Handbook*.

Instruction

Discuss with students the note-taking process. Explain that in order to take good notes students must be able to identify what information is most important. Review with the class how to identify the main idea. (For a more detailed review, see pages 106–107 of the handbook.) Explain that their notes should focus on the main idea and the details that support it. Remind students not to use too many quotes in their notes.

Teaching Approach

Use of the Handbook

Have students work in pairs to read page 98. Encourage partners to pay close attention to the sample Study Cards.

Extend the Handbook

Ask students to practice creating Study Cards using the chapter of the geography textbook from previous lessons. Encourage them to come up with three or four questions to answer. Remind them that the questions should reflect the main idea(s) of the chapter. Discuss how creating the Study Cards affected their understanding of the material.

For more practice, see pages 29–38 of the *Student Applications Book 6*.

Assessment
Ask students:

■ What is the purpose of taking notes?

■ How do you know what information to include when taking notes?

■ How can taking notes help you read a geography textbook?

WEEK 8
Lesson 8
Reading Geography: A Review

For use with *Reader's Handbook* pages 84–99

Goals

In this lesson, students review what they learned in this unit and apply After Reading activities to help them better understand and retain the information.

Teaching Focus

Background

Now that students have a basic understanding of two strategies available for reading geography, a review of the unit as a whole will help them retain the information and transfer it to other geography reading experiences.

Instruction

Review with the class the strategies and tools learned in this unit. You might create an Outline on the board, listing the three stages of the reading process and the steps for reading geography that fall under each stage.

Teaching Approach

Use of the Handbook

To help them review and remember the information in this lesson, have students apply the After Reading activities discussed in Lesson 6. First, encourage them to pause and reflect on the lesson. What did they learn from reading it? Are there parts of the text that they found difficult? Have them reread any parts that they still don't quite understand. To conclude the review process, have them work with a partner to create a few Study Cards for the lesson.

Extend the Handbook

Have students work in small groups to apply the strategies they learned in this unit to another chapter in the geography textbook. Remind them to refer to the Outline from the board or the copy in their textbooks.

Assessment

Ask students:

■ How did applying the reading process affect your understanding of the reading?

■ What is the most important thing you learned in this lesson? Explain your answer.

WEEK 9

Elements of Textbooks

For use with *Reader's Handbook* pages 155–169

Daily Lessons	Summary*
Lesson 1 **Features of Textbooks**	Discuss with the class the common characteristics of textbook chapters, including boldface terms, headings, and previews.
Lesson 2 **Textbook Graphics**	Work with students to explore the various non-text features of textbooks, including charts, graphs, maps, photos, and illustrations.
Lesson 3 **Textbook Glossaries**	Have students examine glossaries and discuss their purposes. Have students also develop a glossary of their own.
Lesson 4 **The Table of Contents and Index**	Discuss with the class two more features of textbooks—the table of contents and index. Help students recognize the purposes of each.

*Use these notes to help you teach a mini-lesson or to teach a briefer, shorter version of the lessons for more proficient students.

Lesson Resources

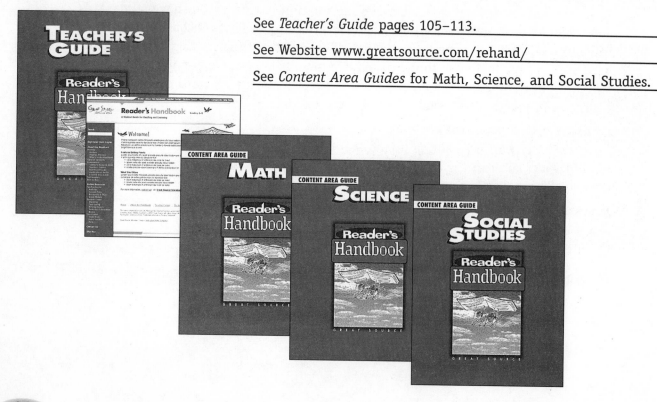

See *Teacher's Guide* pages 105–113.

See Website www.greatsource.com/rehand/

See *Content Area Guides* for Math, Science, and Social Studies.

84

WEEK 10

Elements of Nonfiction

For use with *Reader's Handbook* pages 273–291

Daily Lessons	Summary*
Lesson 1 **Chronological Order**	Work with students to explore texts structured in chronological order. Discuss as a class the importance of understanding text structure when reading nonfiction.
Lesson 2 **Problem and Solution**	Build understanding of nonfiction writing that utilizes a problem-solution text structure.
Lesson 3 **Fact and Opinion**	Discuss with students the differences between facts and opinions and why it is important to evaluate both when reading nonfiction.
Lesson 4 **Connotation and Denotation**	Help students understand the difference between a word's connotation and its denotation.

*Use these notes to help you teach a mini-lesson or to teach a briefer, shorter version of the lessons for more proficient students.

Lesson Resources

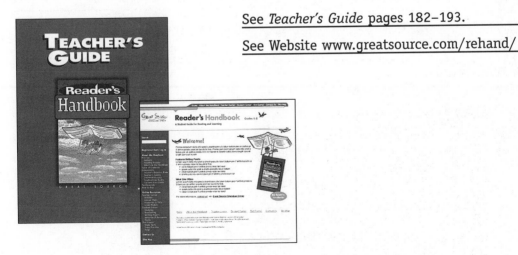

See *Teacher's Guide* pages 182–193.

See Website www.greatsource.com/rehand/

WEEK 9
Lesson 1 ▸ Features of Textbook Chapters

For use with *Reader's Handbook* pages 156, 160–161, 166–167

Goals

In this lesson, students examine common features found in textbook chapters, including boldface terms, headings and titles, and previews.

Teaching Focus

Background

Textbooks across the curriculum share certain characteristics. Examining the common features of a typical textbook chapter will help students use these features to better understand their reading.

Instruction

Gather a collection of different textbooks. Randomly pass them out to students or small groups of students. Have students skim through one chapter and list its features. Discuss the similarities and differences among the books. Explain that no matter what the subject, most textbooks share common features, including boldface terms, headings, previews, and study questions.

Teaching Approach

Use of the Handbook

Break the class into three groups. Assign each of the groups one of the following: *boldface terms* (page 156), *headings* and *titles* (pages 160–161), *preview* (pages 166–167). Ask groups to "teach" their textbook feature to the rest of the class. Then discuss as a whole class how each of these features can help students better understand their reading.

Extend the Handbook

Have students work as partners to examine their textbooks. Ask partners to make a chart listing the three features discussed above across the top and the names of the textbooks down the left side. Have students fill in the chart by noting which textbooks contain the different features. Encourage partners to write a summary of their findings.

Assessment

Ask students:

■ What are three common features of textbook chapters?

■ Why do you think authors of textbooks include these features?

■ Why is it important to pay attention to these features?

WEEK 9
Lesson 2 Textbook Graphics

For use with *Reader's Handbook* pages 157, 159, 163–165

Goals

In this lesson, students explore the various nontext features of textbooks, including charts, graphs, maps, photos, and illustrations.

Teaching Focus

Background

Nontext features of textbooks—which include charts, graphs, maps, photos, and illustrations—add visual appeal to the material. These graphics also provide visual clues about the text and often contain important information not found in the text. Graphics are particularly beneficial to visual learners.

Instruction

Discuss the phrase "a picture is worth a thousand words." Explain that textbooks contain pictures and other graphic aids that emphasize points about a subject. Have students skim class textbooks to explore the types of graphics used in textbooks. Explain that in this lesson they will learn more about four types of graphics: charts, graphs, maps, and photos and illustrations.

Teaching Approach

Use of the Handbook

Divide the class into four groups. Assign each group one of the following: *charts* (page 157), *graphs* (page 159), *maps* (pages 163–164), and *photos* and *illustrations* (page 165). Have each group share what they learned about the graphic with the rest of the class.

Extend the Handbook

Ask students to reflect on one of the graphics commonly used in textbooks. Have them look through one of their textbooks for examples of the graphic. Then encourage them to jot down their thoughts about the graphic. What is its purpose? What information does it contain?

Assessment

Ask students:

■ What are four kinds of graphics commonly found in textbooks?

■ Why do you think textbooks contain these types of graphics?

■ Has this lesson changed the way you interpret textbook graphics? Why or why not?

WEEK 9
Lesson 3 — Textbook Glossaries

For use with *Reader's Handbook* page 158

Goals

In this lesson, students examine glossaries and their purposes.

Teaching Focus

Background

Proficient readers know that glossaries are wonderful tools for understanding unfamiliar terminology. While some students recognize the usefulness of glossaries and rely on them when reading difficult material, others may be less familiar with them. These students will benefit from explicit instruction in their use.

Instruction

Gather a supply of textbooks for students to peruse. Have them check the back of the textbooks to see which of them contain glossaries. After allowing them time to examine the glossaries, discuss with students why they think some textbooks include glossaries. What purpose do they serve?

Teaching Approach

Use of the Handbook

Read aloud the first paragraph on page 158. Then work through the example with the class. Ask a volunteer to read the information under Description. Discuss the relationship between this section of the *Reader's Handbook* and a glossary. Lead students to see that glossaries don't always have to be in the back of a book; sections such as this can be considered glossaries as well.

Extend the Handbook

Have students work in pairs to develop a glossary of their own. Ask them to skim a chapter of a classroom textbook and jot down words they think should be included in the glossary. When they're finished, have them compare their list to the actual glossary in the book. Alternatively, if no glossary exists, encourage them to write brief definitions for their words to use as a mini-glossary for the textbook.

Assessment

Ask students:

■ What is a glossary?

■ Why do textbooks include glossaries?

■ How might a glossary be helpful to you when you're reading textbooks?

WEEK 9
Lesson 4 — The Table of Contents and Index

For use with *Reader's Handbook* pages 162 and 168–169

Goals

In this lesson, students learn about two more features of textbooks: the table of contents and the index.

Teaching Focus

Background
The table of contents and index are main stays of practically all textbooks, and proficient readers know when and how to use each. Recognizing the similarities and differences between these two features will help students use them more effectively.

Instruction
Ask students what they know about the table of contents and index. How are they similar? How are they different? Create a Venn Diagram to help organize the discussion. Lead students to see that while both are useful resources for finding information in a textbook, a table of contents helps readers find broad topics and an index lists specific topics, terms, people, and places.

See page 683 of the *Reader's Handbook* for more information on Venn Diagrams.

Teaching Approach

Use of the Handbook
Work through page 162 with the class. Examine the comparison between an index and a search engine. (Suggest that students review page 533.) Then have students read pages 168–169 independently. Discuss with the class what they learned from their reading. Add to or modify the Venn Diagram as necessary.

Extend the Handbook
Call out topics or terms from a class textbook. Ask students if they would look for the topic in the table of contents of a textbook or its index. Have them explain their answers.

Assessment
Ask students:

■ What do the table of contents and the index have in common? How are they different?

■ How do you know which feature to use when you are trying to find information in a textbook?

WEEK 10
Lesson 1 ▸ Chronological Order

For use with *Reader's Handbook* page 276

Goals

In this lesson, students examine chronological order and how it can be used in nonfiction writing.

Teaching Focus

Background

Understanding the various text structures found in nonfiction provides a recognizable framework that helps students make sense of their reading. Students proficient in identifying these text structures will also begin applying them more efficiently in their own writing. Here chronological order, one of the more familiar structures, is examined.

Instruction

Write the following words on the board: *first, next, then, later, finally.* Ask students what all these words have in common. Lead students to see that these words all have to do with sequence. Brainstorm with the class other sequence words. Explain that coming across words such as these in nonfiction materials is often an indication that the material is written in chronological order. Point out that determining how a piece of writing is put together, or *structured*, will help them keep track of information.

Teaching Approach

Use of the Handbook

Have students work in small groups to read and discuss the information on page 276 of the *Reader's Handbook*. You might also have groups read about Timelines on page 681 of the handbook and discuss why using a Timeline would be helpful when reading information presented in chronological order.

Extend the Handbook

Ask students to write a short piece in chronological order. They might consider topics such as how to make a peanut butter and jelly sandwich or what they did yesterday after school. Encourage them to first plan their piece by creating a Timeline or Storyboard of events.

Assessment

Ask students:

■ Why is it important to know how a piece of writing is structured?

■ How can you tell if something is written in chronological order?

WEEK 10
Lesson 2 · Problem and Solution

For use with *Reader's Handbook* page 286

Goals

In this lesson, students examine nonfiction text structured in a problem and solution format.

Teaching Focus

Background

Problem and solution order is another way in which nonfiction writing can be organized. As stated in the previous lesson, recognizing how a piece of writing is organized enables readers to more easily access information. It helps them mentally "map" a selection.

Instruction

Discuss with students the relationship between a problem and its solution(s). Explain that sometimes authors organize their writing around a problem and its solutions or possible solutions. Discuss with the class situations in which an author might want to use this type of structure. Then discuss why it is important for readers to be able to identify problem and solution structure when they read.

Teaching Approach

Use of the Handbook

Read aloud the paragraphs in the example on page 286 of the *Reader's Handbook*. Think aloud as you read, calling attention to the problem and its solution. Work with the class to develop a problem and at solution chart to help organize the information in the example. Then have a student volunteer read the description and definition of problem-solution text structure.

Extend the Handbook

Ask students to write a paragraph or two using a problem-solution order. Encourage them to think about a problem they've had at home or at school and how they solved it. They might begin by organizing their information in a problem and solution chart such as the one they created above.

Assessment

Ask students:

■ How can you tell if something is written using a problem-solution organization?

■ How does knowing that a piece of writing is organized around a problem and solution help you as the reader?

■ Do you think it is easier to recognize chronological or problem-solution organization? Explain.

WEEK 10
Lesson 3 — Fact and Opinion

For use with *Reader's Handbook* page 281

Goals

In this lesson, students learn how to distinguish between fact and opinion and why it is important to do so when reading nonfiction.

Teaching Focus

Background

The ability to differentiate between facts and opinions is a critical skill when reading nonfiction material. Proficient readers understand that even the most seemingly objective material often includes opinions. Separating fact from opinion is necessary in order to evaluate the material effectively.

Instruction

Discuss with students the difference between facts and opinions. How can students determine if something is a fact or not? Explain that a fact is a statement that can be proven true. Ask volunteers for examples of facts. Then discuss opinions. Explain that an opinion is one person's view; it cannot be proven true or false. Again ask for examples. Discuss why it is important to separate facts from opinions when students read nonfiction.

Teaching Approach

Use of the Handbook

Read aloud the Example on page 281. Think aloud as you read, focusing on how you separate the facts and opinions in the material. Then have a student volunteer read aloud the Description and Definition of *fact* and *opinion*. Discuss what it means to "evaluate the facts and opinions as you read." Point out that this is just what you did as you read the sample aloud.

Extend the Handbook

Have students work in pairs to peruse magazine or newspaper articles for examples of facts and opinions. Encourage them to list the facts and opinions, then evaluate them by asking themselves, "Are the opinions well supported? Are the facts from reliable sources?" Have students share their findings with the rest of the class.

Assessment

Ask students:

■ What is the difference between a fact and an opinion?

■ Why is it important to know the difference between fact and opinion?

WEEK 10
Lesson 4 Connotation and Denotation

For use with *Reader's Handbook* page 279

Goals

In this lesson, students examine the difference between a word's connotation and its denotation and why it is important to recognize this difference when reading nonfiction.

Teaching Focus

Background

Every word has both a *denotation*, its dictionary definition, and a *connotation*, the emotions people associate with the word. Recognizing the difference between the two and understanding how authors can use a word's connotation, in particular, to send a message to the reader enable us to evaluate the material more effectively.

Instruction

Ask students what the difference is between *young* and *childish* or between *shack* and *cottage*. What images do the different words suggest? Explain that certain words can have very similar *denotations*, or dictionary definitions, but these same words can have very different *connotations*, or feelings that people attach to them. Explain that an author's choice of words can affect a reader's feelings about a subject. Discuss why it is important to be aware of an author's use of connotation when reading nonfiction.

Teaching Approach

Use of the Handbook

The distinction between connotation and denotation is sometimes quite subtle; understanding the distinction can be difficult at first for some students. Therefore, if possible, work with small groups to read and discuss page 279 of the *Reader's Handbook*. Encourage students to share their questions about the material.

Extend the Handbook

Ask small groups to skim magazine or newspaper articles for examples of connotations. Have the group discuss why the author might have chosen a certain word. What feelings do students associate with the word?

Assessment

Ask students:

■ What is the difference between denotation and connotation?

■ Why is it important to recognize the difference between a word's connotation and its denotation?

WEEK 11

Reading Biographies and Autobiographies

For use with *Reader's Handbook* pages 188–217

Daily Lessons	Summary*
Lesson 1 **Biographies and** **Autobiographies:** **An Overview**	Review with students how to set a purpose, preview, and plan for reading this section of the *Reader's Handbook*.
Lesson 2 **Before Reading** **a Biography**	Review the Before Reading steps used in Lesson 1. Apply them to reading a biography.
Lesson 3 **How Biographies** **Are Organized**	Work with students to examine the organization of biographies. Discuss the use of chronological order in biographies.
Lesson 4 **Biographies and** **Reading Tools**	Help students identify the various tools they might use to keep track of information in a biography.

*Use these notes to help you teach a mini-lesson or to teach a briefer, shorter version of the lessons for more proficient students.

Lesson Resources

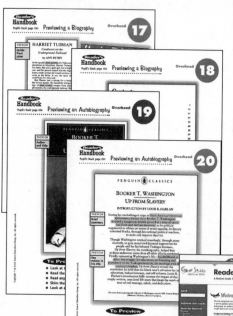

Overheads

For this lesson, use:

Overheads 17 and 18: Previewing a Biography
Overheads 19 and 20: Previewing an Autobiography

See *Student Applications Book 6* pages 72–89.

See *Teacher's Guide* pages 127–147.

See Website www.greatsource.com/rehand/

For more practice, see also *Sourcebook* Grade 6, pages 122–130, 131–140, 202–212; *Daybook* Grade 6, pages 121–122, 189–193, 216–217.

Reading Biographies and Autobiographies
(continued)

For use with *Reader's Handbook* pages 188–217

Daily Lessons	Summary*
Lesson 5 **Reading an Autobiography**	Have students apply the three stages of the reading process to reading an autobiography.
Lesson 6 **Reading Strategy: Synthesizing**	Help students understand what synthesizing is and why it is an important skill for reading autobiographies.
Lesson 7 **Biographies, Autobiographies, and Their Subjects**	Lead students to understand that the main purpose of biographies and autobiographies is to explore a person's life and its meaning.
Lesson 8 **Evaluating Biographies and Autobiographies**	Discuss the importance of evaluating the facts in biographies and autobiographies for accuracy.

*Use these notes to help you teach a mini-lesson or to teach a briefer, shorter version of the lessons for more proficient students.

Lesson Resources

Overheads

For this lesson, use:

Overheads 17 and 18: Previewing a Biography

Overheads 19 and 20: Previewing an Autobiography

See *Student Applications Book 6* pages 72–89.

See *Teacher's Guide* pages 127–147.

See Website www.greatsource.com/rehand/

For more practice, see also *Sourcebook* Grade 6, pages 122–130, 131–140, 202–212; *Daybook* Grade 6, pages 121–122, 189–193, 216–217.

WEEK 11
Lesson 1

Biographies and Autobiographies: An Overview

For use with *Reader's Handbook* pages 188–217

Goals

In this lesson, students practice Before Reading steps to set a purpose, preview, and plan for reading this section of the *Reader's Handbook*.

Teaching Focus

Background

Throughout the handbook, students are urged to set a purpose, preview, and plan before reading. Have them practice these steps as they prepare to read this section of the *Reader's Handbook*.

Instruction

Activate prior knowledge by discussing with students what they know about biographies and autobiographies. Ask them to share the subjects of any biographies and autobiographies they have read and enjoyed. Explain that in this unit they will be learning more about these two genres, including how they are organized and what reading strategies work well with them. Work with the class to set purposes for reading this section of the handbook.

Teaching Approach

Use of the Handbook

Have students work in pairs to preview pages 188–217. First, review the previewing process. Encourage students to pay attention to headings, lists, and graphics. After previewing, have partners discuss their plan for reading.

Extend the Handbook

Now that they've previewed this section, encourage students to jot down their thoughts about biographies and autobiographies. What questions do they have about these genres? Do they enjoy reading them? Why or why not? Have volunteers share their responses.

Assessment

Ask students:

■ What is your purpose for reading this section of the *Reader's Handbook*?

■ What did you learn from previewing it?

■ What would you like to learn about biographies and autobiographies?

WEEK 11
Lesson 2 Before Reading a Biography

For use with *Reader's Handbook* pages 188–192

Goals

In this lesson, students apply the steps in Before Reading to a biography.

Teaching Focus

Background
Proficient readers recognize the importance of utilizing the steps in prereading. In order for students to truly integrate these steps into their reading experiences, they need repeated practice and step-by-step support. In this lesson, students are guided through the processes of setting a purpose, previewing, and planning as they relate to reading biographies.

Instruction
Review with students the Before Reading steps of setting a purpose, previewing, and planning. Explain that in this lesson they will learn ways to apply these general activities before reading a biography. What do students think a purpose might be for reading a biography?

Teaching Approach

Use of the Handbook
Read aloud page 188 of the *Reader's Handbook*. Review the purposes listed on page 189. How do they compare to those discussed in class? Then have students work in small groups to read and discuss the previewing section on pages 189–192. Discuss how previewing a biography compares to previewing other materials. Ask a student volunteer to read aloud the top of page 192 on planning to read a biography.

Extend the Handbook
Gather a supply of biographies for students to work with. Have partners or small groups choose one to preview. Encourage groups to discuss what they learn from previewing.

For more practice, see pages 72–79 of the *Student Applications Book 6*.

Assessment
Ask students:

■ How is the purpose for reading a biography different from the purpose for reading other types of nonfiction? How is it the same?

■ Why is it important to set a purpose, preview, and plan before reading a biography?

WEEK 11
Lesson 3
How Biographies Are Organized

For use with *Reader's Handbook* pages 196–199

Goals

In this lesson, students examine the organization of biographies to help them keep track of information.

Teaching Focus

Background

Biographies share certain common characteristics, one of which is their organization. Most biographies are organized in a linear, time-order fashion. Recognizing this structure will help students track information as they read.

Instruction

Review with students the characteristics of chronological order. (See page 197 of the *Reader's Handbook* for a detailed review.) Explain that most biographies are organized in this way. Discuss why authors of biographies choose to organize their writing in chronological order.

Teaching Approach

Use of the Handbook

Read aloud the bottom of page 196 of the *Reader's Handbook*. Then divide the class into small groups to read and discuss the information on pages 197–199. Come together as a class and review the material. Ask student volunteers to share what they learned about the four types of details to look for when reading a biography.

Extend the Handbook

Have partners or small groups return to the biographies they previewed in the last lesson. Ask them to skim through a chapter or two to get a sense of how the biography is organized. Encourage students to look for clue words that indicate changes in time, such as those listed on page 197 of the handbook.

For more practice, see pages 72–79 of the *Student Applications Book 6*.

Assessment

Ask students:

■ What are four kinds of details to look for when reading a biography?

■ Why are these details important?

■ How can knowing the organization of biographies help you understand the material?

WEEK 11
Lesson 4 Biographies and Reading Tools

For use with *Reader's Handbook* pages 188–203

Goals

In this lesson, students learn how various reading tools can be used to get the most out of reading biographies.

Teaching Focus

Background

Biographies, because they are generally written in chronological order, are obviously well suited to Timelines. But there are other graphic organizers that work well with biographies, several of which are discussed in this section of the handbook. Familiarizing themselves with these organizers and understanding when to use each will help students construct meaning from biographical texts.

Instruction

Point out to students that four main types of tools will be described in this section of the handbook: Cause-Effect Organizer, Timeline, Character Map, and Outline. Explain that each of these tools has a different purpose. In order to know which tool to use when reading a biography, or any piece of nonfiction, readers need to know its purpose.

Teaching Approach

Use of the Handbook

Divide the class into four groups. Assign one of the following to each: Cause-Effect Organizer (page 192), Timeline (page 198), Character Map (page 199), Outline (page 202). Have each group discuss the purpose of their tool. When would they use this tool? What information will the tool provide? Ask groups to summarize their findings for the rest of the class.

For more information on these tools, see the Reader's Almanac in the back of the *Reader's Handbook*.

Extend the Handbook

Have students read a chapter from the biography they used in the previous lessons. Encourage them to use a reading tool to keep track of their reading.

Assessment

Ask students:

■ How can reading tools help you understand information in a biography?

■ Which tool are you most comfortable using? Why?

WEEK 12
Lesson 5 — Reading an Autobiography

For use with *Reader's Handbook* pages 204–217

Goals

In this lesson, students apply the reading process to reading autobiographies.

Teaching Focus

Background

Biographies and autobiographies share many of the same features; thus, the technique used for reading a biography can also be applied to reading an autobiography. This lesson reviews the activities learned for reading biographies and expands them to include reading autobiographies.

Instruction

Ask student volunteers to define an autobiography. Lead students to see that autobiographies are much like biographies, except that in an autobiography the author writes about his or her own life. Explain that readers can use many of the same strategies and tools for reading autobiographies that they use when reading biographies. Review with students some of the strategies and tools they learned about in the previous lessons.

Teaching Approach

Use of the Handbook

As a whole class, work through pages 204–208 of the *Reader's Handbook*. Discuss how the purposes of autobiographies compare to those of biographies. Then have students read pages 210–214 independently. Encourage them to keep their purpose for reading in mind. Come together as a class and discuss the After Reading strategies on pages 215–217.

Extend the Handbook

Ask students to reflect on this lesson in their journals. They might use questions such as the following as a guide: What steps did I complete most easily? Which one do I have the most difficulty applying to an autobiography? What can I do to help myself more effectively the next time I read an autobiography?

For more practice, see pages 80–89 of the *Student Applications Book 6*.

Assessment

Ask students:

■ What is an autobiography?

■ How will you use this lesson the next time you read an autobiography?

WEEK 12
Lesson 6
Reading Strategy: Synthesizing

For use with *Reader's Handbook* pages 208–209

Goals

In this lesson, students learn how synthesizing information can help enhance their understanding of an autobiography.

Teaching Focus

Background

Synthesizing is one of the more complex reading strategies, and some students may have trouble grasping it at first. But synthesizing is also one of the most important reading strategies, and proficient readers rely on it without even realizing it in almost every reading situation. Synthesizing is a critical skill for reading autobiographies because we need to take the bits and pieces of information we receive about the subject and put them all together.

Instruction

Explain to students that to synthesize information, readers fit together small pieces of data to form a whole concept, much like putting together the pieces of a jigsaw puzzle. Explain that in this section of the handbook, students will learn more about synthesizing and why it is an important strategy to use when reading an autobiography.

Teaching Approach

Use of the Handbook

Read aloud the information on the bottom of page 208 of the *Reader's Handbook*. Then work with the class to examine the Key Topic Notes on page 209. Discuss the usefulness of the organizer. Remind students that while they would create their Key Topic Notes before reading, they would fill it in during reading.

For more information on synthesizing, see pages 660–661 of the *Reader's Handbook*.

Extend the Handbook

Have students use their journals to reflect on the lesson. What have they learned about synthesizing? What questions do they still have? When would they use Key Topic Notes?

Assessment

Ask students:

■ What does it mean to synthesize information?

■ Why is it important to synthesize information when you read an autobiography?

WEEK 12
Lesson 7 Biographies, Autobiographies, and Their Subjects

For use with *Reader's Handbook* pages 188–217

Goals

In this lesson, students consider the main focus of biographies and autobiographies: exploring a person's life and its meaning.

Teaching Focus

Background

Understanding Before and After Reading steps, learning how to use graphic organizers, synthesizing—these are all important tools for reading biographies and autobiographies. But at the heart of reading both genres is a desire to learn the details of a person's life. Focusing on techniques biographers and autobiographers use to bring their subjects to life will help students get a better sense of the primary focus of biographies and autobiographies.

Instruction

Discuss with students how authors choose the subjects for their biographies. Explain that the underlying purpose of every biography is to describe a subject's life in detail. Point out that autobiographies have a similar purpose.

Teaching Approach

Use of the Handbook

Review the section on setting purposes for reading biographies (page 189) and autobiographies (page 205). Then, review the Character Map on page 199, the Character Trait Web on page 212, and the Inference Chart on page 214. Discuss how all these reading tools can be used to help readers understand the subjects of biographies and autobiographies.

Extend the Handbook

Have students create and use one of the graphic organizers listed above to explore the subject of a biography or an autobiography that they have read. Encourage them to summarize the information in the graphic by writing one or two sentences about the subject.

Assessment

Ask students:

■ What is the main purpose of biographies and autobiographies?

■ Why is it important to keep this purpose in mind when you read biographies and autobiographies?

WEEK 12
Lesson 8
Evaluating Biographies and Autobiographies

For use with *Reader's Handbook* pages 188–217

Goals

In this lesson, students compare the similarities and differences between biographies and autobiographies and discuss the importance of evaluating the information in each.

Teaching Focus

Background

While biographies and autobiographies share many similar features, students need to keep in mind the key distinction between the two genres. Biographies are written by an objective (or at least a seemingly objective) outside party, while autobiographies are written by the subjects themselves. Proficient readers recognize that *who* writes the material can affect its accuracy and point of view.

Instruction

Discuss with students the similarities and differences between biographies and autobiographies. Lead students to see that the main difference between the two involves who is doing the writing. Discuss the advantages and disadvantages of each genre. Explain that readers need to evaluate carefully the facts in biographies and autobiographies to make sure what the author tells them is fair and accurate.

Teaching Approach

Use of the Handbook

Divide the class into two groups. Have one group reread the biography excerpt on pages 193–195. Ask the other group to reread the autobiographical excerpt on pages 210–211. Encourage each group to evaluate the excerpt. Do they think the writing is objective? Is it insightful? Have groups summarize their discussions and share their thoughts.

Extend the Handbook

Have students write autobiographical sketches of an important time in their lives. Ask them to evaluate their own work by asking themselves questions such as these: Is this an accurate portrayal of the experience? Have I left anything of importance out?

Assessment

Ask students:

■ Why should you evaluate the facts in a biography or autobiography?

■ Which genre do you think contains a more well-rounded view of a person? Explain.

Reading a Newspaper Article

For use with *Reader's Handbook* pages 218–233

Daily Lessons	Summary*
Lesson 1 **How and Why We Read Newspaper Articles**	Have students examine the reasons for reading newspapers and strategies they can use for reading them.
Lesson 2 **The Lead and the 5 W's**	Explain to students what a lead is and discuss the five key questions newspaper articles answer—*who, what, where, when,* and *why.*
Lesson 3 **Reading Strategy: Reading Critically**	Work with students to explore the strategy of reading critically. Discuss how it can help them evaluate the information in a newspaper article.
Lesson 4 **How Newspaper Articles Are Organized**	Help students identify how newspaper articles can be organized with an inverted pyramid structure.

*Use these notes to help you teach a mini-lesson or to teach a briefer, shorter version of the lessons for more proficient students.

Lesson Resources

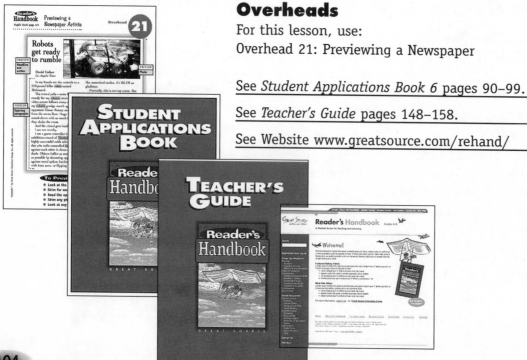

Overheads

For this lesson, use:
Overhead 21: Previewing a Newspaper

See *Student Applications Book 6* pages 90–99.

See *Teacher's Guide* pages 148–158.

See Website www.greatsource.com/rehand/

WEEK 14

Focus on Persuasive Writing

For use with *Reader's Handbook* pages 247–255, 280

Daily Lessons	Summary*
Lesson 1 **Characteristics of Persuasive Writing**	Discuss with students the characteristics of persuasive writing. Have students apply the first two stages of the reading process to a persuasive piece.
Lesson 2 **The Three Parts of an Argument**	Work with students to explore the three parts of an effective argument—the author's viewpoint, supporting details, and the opposing viewpoint.
Lesson 3 **After Reading Persuasive Writing**	Have students examine how and why to apply the After Reading steps to persuasive writing.
Lesson 4 **Editorials**	Help students understand how to evaluate a newspaper editorial.

*Use these notes to help you teach a mini-lesson or to teach a briefer, shorter version of the lessons for more proficient students.

Lesson Resources

See *Student Applications Book 6* pages 109–111.

See *Teacher's Guide* pages 170–173.

See Website www.greatsource.com/rehand/

For more practice, see also *Daybook* Grade 6, pages 200–201.

WEEK 13
Lesson 1
How and Why We Read Newspaper Articles

For use with *Reader's Handbook* pages 218–233

Goals

In this lesson, students explore newspaper articles and the strategies that can be used to read them.

Teaching Focus

Background

Newspapers are valuable reference sources, something many of us rely on each day for information and entertainment. Newspapers can be overwhelming for students, however, if they don't realize that they are not expected to read every word of every article. A discussion of what newspapers have to offer and strategies for reading them will enable students to get the most out of the material.

Instruction

Pass out newspapers for students to browse through, and ask them to note the kinds of information newspapers contain. Discuss with the class why people read newspapers. Explain that each person reads the newspaper differently because a reader's purpose affects how and what the reader chooses to read. Lead students to see that newspapers are not meant to be read front to back, word for word; instead, readers select which articles to read based on their purposes for reading.

Teaching Approach

Use of the Handbook

Read aloud page 218 of the *Reader's Handbook*. Then have students work in pairs to read and discuss the Before Reading steps on pages 219–223. Ask students to read pages 224–227 to see how During Reading steps can be applied to newspaper articles. As a class, work through the After Reading steps on pages 231–233.

Extend the Handbook

Have students choose an article from one of the newspapers used earlier. Ask them to apply three of the strategies learned in this section of the handbook to the article. Discuss how using these strategies affected their understanding.

For more practice, see pages 90–99 of the *Student Applications Book 6*.

Assessment

Ask students:

■ What is one purpose for reading newspapers?

■ What strategy did you find most helpful for reading the newspaper article? Why?

WEEK 13
Lesson 2 — The Lead and the 5 W's

For use with *Reader's Handbook* pages 220, 280

Goals

In this lesson, students learn what leads are and the five questions that good leads answer.

Teaching Focus

Background

The 5 W's—*who, what, when, where, why*—are the key questions a newspaper article needs to answer. Proficient readers know to keep these questions in mind as they read. They also understand that an article's lead paragraph usually answers, or begins to answer, these questions. Understanding what these five questions are and where to find answers to them will help students get the most out of newspaper articles.

Instruction

Explain to students that there are five critical questions a newspaper article should answer. Discuss with students what these five questions are and why each is important. Then explain that readers can usually find the answers to these questions in the very first paragraph of the article, called the lead. Discuss the purpose of a lead. Point out that because newspapers contain so much information, readers can read lead paragraphs to get the essence of most articles.

Teaching Approach

Use of the Handbook

Read aloud the example lead on page 280 of the *Reader's Handbook*. Think aloud as you read, focusing on how the lead answers the 5 W's. Have volunteers read aloud the rest of page 280. Then have students read page 220 on their own.

Extend the Handbook

Have students write a lead paragraph for a newspaper article. They might choose to write about a local event, a school activity, or a noteworthy person. Ask them to begin by creating a 5 W's Organizer such as the one on page 220 of the handbook. Encourage students to share their leads with a partner. Can partners find the answers to the 5 W's in each other's leads?

Assessment

Ask students:

■ What is the purpose of a lead paragraph in a newspaper article?

■ What are the 5 W's?

■ How does answering the 5 W's help you better understand the information in an article?

WEEK 13
Lesson 3 Reading Strategy: Reading Critically

For use with *Reader's Handbook* pages 222–223, 228

Goals

In this lesson, students explore the strategy of critical reading and discover how it can help them evaluate the information in a newspaper article.

Teaching Focus

Background

Newspaper articles demand critical reading. Proficient readers continually evaluate the information as they read to determine its fairness and accuracy. Some articles are biased, presenting opinions as facts or leaving out information that supports the other side of an issue. In order to be able to evaluate the material effectively, students need step-by-step guidance in critical reading.

Instruction

Discuss why it is important for readers to evaluate what they read in a newspaper article. Lead students to see that not all newspaper articles are accurate. Some of them might state an opinion as fact, use unreliable sources for their information, or simply have not told both sides of the whole story. Explain that active readers read newspaper articles critically. Discuss with students what they think it means to *read critically*.

Teaching Approach

Use of the Handbook

Read aloud the bottom of page 222. Then work through the Critical Reading Charts on pages 223 and 228 with students. Explain that answering these questions as they read an article will help them evaluate the information.

Extend the Handbook

Have small groups of students apply the reading strategy of reading critically to another newspaper article. Encourage groups to discuss the five critical reading questions as they read. Do groups think the article contains fair and accurate information? Ask them to share their findings with the rest of the class.

Assessment

Ask students:

■ What are the five critical reading questions to ask when reading a newspaper article?

■ Why is it important to ask these questions?

WEEK 13
Lesson 4 How Newspaper Articles Are Organized

For use with *Reader's Handbook* page 229

Goals

In this lesson, students explore how newspaper articles can be organized with an inverted pyramid.

Teaching Focus

Background

Evaluating the information in a newspaper article is more easily accomplished once readers recognize how the article is constructed. By exploring a common structure—the inverted pyramid—students will begin to understand that many newspaper articles are organized in similar ways.

Instruction

Discuss with students why it helps to know how a newspaper article is organized. Explain that many articles are organized in similar ways. Point out that in this lesson students will learn about one common format for newspaper articles.

Teaching Approach

Use of the Handbook

Ask a student volunteer to read the first paragraph on page 229. Discuss the inverted pyramid pattern. Then work with the class to read the bottom half of page 229 and to reread the first few paragraphs on page 221. Do students think the buried lead is an effective opening?

Extend the Handbook

Have students work in small groups to skim newspaper articles, looking for examples of the inverted pyramid. Ask groups to keep track of the number of articles they find that are organized in this way. What conclusions can they draw from their tally?

Assessment

Ask students:

■ What are the key features of the inverted pyramid for organizing newspaper articles?

■ Why do you think writers might organize a newspaper article using the inverted pyramid structure?

WEEK 14
Lesson 1 — Characteristics of Persuasive Writing

For use with *Reader's Handbook* pages 247–255

Goals

In this lesson, students discuss the characteristics of persuasive writing and apply the first two stages of the reading process to a persuasive piece.

Teaching Focus

Background

Most proficient readers recognize the importance of applying critical reading strategies to persuasive writing. Less experienced readers, however, may not recognize persuasive writing when they see it; moreover, they may not understand the importance of reading such pieces critically. For this reason, many students will benefit from a step-by-step application of the reading process to persuasive writing.

Instruction

Ask student volunteers to tell what they know about persuasive writing. Work with the class to list characteristics of persuasive writing, such as supporting a cause, expressing an opinion, and presenting an argument. Explain that in this lesson students will see how they can use the steps in the reading process to understand and evaluate persuasive writing.

Teaching Approach

Use of the Handbook

Read aloud the top of page 247 in the *Reader's Handbook*. Discuss the three goals of the section. Then ask students to work with a partner to read page 249 to learn how to apply the strategy of reading critically to persuasive writing. To see how this strategy works, invite students to read the editorial on pages 250–252 independently.

Extend the Handbook

Ask students to reflect on this section of the *Reader's Handbook* in their journals. Questions they might consider: What strategies did I use most easily? Which one do I have the most difficulty applying to persuasive writing? How can I use this strategy more effectively the next time I read persuasive writing?

For more practice, see pages 109–111 of the *Student Applications Book 6*.

Assessment

Ask students:

■ What is the purpose of persuasive writing?

■ How will you use this lesson the next time you read a persuasive piece?

WEEK 14
Lesson 2
The Three Parts of an Argument

For use with *Reader's Handbook* pages 249–253

Goals

In this lesson, students explore the three parts of an effective argument—the author's viewpoint, supporting details, and the opposing viewpoint.

Teaching Focus

Background

A well-composed argument is made up of three parts—the author's viewpoint, details that support that viewpoint, and a mention of the opposing viewpoint(s). In order to effectively evaluate an argument, readers must be able to identify these three parts of an argument and also understand that if any of these parts is missing, the argument is flawed.

Instruction

Ask volunteers to describe what they do when they try to convince their parents of something. Do they state their opinion? Give reasons why their parents should agree with them? Explain to students that all good arguments consist of three parts—the author's or speaker's opinion, reasons why others should agree with the opinion, and an explanation of why the opposing view is flawed. Discuss why all three parts are important.

Teaching Approach

Use of the Handbook

Read aloud the bottom of page 249 in the handbook. Work through the Argument Chart with students. Then have students reread the editorial on pages 250–252, this time noting the places where the three parts of the argument are found. After reading, work through the Argument Chart on page 253. Ask students how well the author presented his argument.

Extend the Handbook

Gather samples of persuasive writing, such as newspaper editorials or letters to the editor. Have students work with a partner or in small groups to create an Argument Chart. Does the argument contain all three parts? Have students share with the rest of the class their thoughts on how well the argument was crafted.

Assessment

Ask students:

■ What are the three parts of an effective argument?

■ Why is it important to include all three in an argument?

WEEK 14
Lesson 3 After Reading Persuasive Writing

For use with *Reader's Handbook* pages 254–255

Goals

In this lesson, students learn how and why to apply After Reading steps to persuasive writing.

Teaching Focus

Background

Effective evaluation of persuasive writing requires thoughtful analysis of the argument both during and after reading. It is not enough to determine if the argument is a sound one; readers must also decide whether or not they agree with the author's viewpoint. The After Reading steps presented in this lesson will help students reflect on their reading.

Instruction

Discuss with students the After Reading stage of the reading process. (See pages 35–37 of the *Reader's Handbook* if students need a review.) Discuss why it is important to take the time after reading a persuasive piece to think about what was read. Explain that students can use After Reading activities to help them evaluate the material and clarify their own views on the subject.

Teaching Approach

Use of the Handbook

Have students work in small groups to read and discuss the three rereading tips to use after reading on pages 254–255 of the *Reader's Handbook*. Ask them to either write an evaluation of the Mike Royko piece or create an Argument Chart (such as the one on page 255) for it. Discuss how applying these tips affected their understanding of the piece.

Extend the Handbook

Have students read another piece of persuasive writing. When they have finished, ask them to apply the After Reading steps discussed earlier.

For more practice, see pages 109–111 of the *Student Applications Book 6*.

Assessment

Ask students:

■ What are three activities to do after reading persuasive writing?

■ Which of these did you find most useful? Explain.

WEEK 14
Lesson 4   Editorials

For use with *Reader's Handbook* pages 249–255, 280

Goals

In this lesson, students learn about editorials and apply what they've learned in this unit to evaluating them.

Teaching Focus

Background

One of the more common forms of persuasive writing, and one that appears in newspapers every day, is the editorial. Editorials, being short and to the point, offer students the opportunity to apply and integrate the strategies they learned in this unit to a common form of persuasive writing.

Instruction

Explain to students what an editorial is and its purpose. Point out that editorials are a specific type of persuasive writing. Review with students what they learned in this unit about reading persuasive writing, and explain that they will apply the strategies they used throughout the unit to an editorial piece.

Teaching Approach

Use of the Handbook

Have a student volunteer read aloud the excerpt from an editorial on page 280 of the *Reader's Handbook*. Ask students to evaluate the editorial based on what they have learned in the unit. What do they think about the argument? Is it sound? Does the author back up the opinion with credible reasons? Then read the description and definition of an editorial aloud. Return to the example and discuss how well it matches the description.

Extend the Handbook

Have students write brief editorials for the school or local paper. You might first brainstorm with the class some community or school-based issues that they could editorialize. Encourage students to share their editorials with a partner. Ask partners to evaluate each other's work using one of the organizers discussed in this unit— an Argument Chart (page 253) or a reading log (page 255).

Assessment

Ask students:

■ What is an editorial?

■ How are editorials similar to other forms of persuasive writing? What sets them apart?

■ What is the most important thing you learned in this unit? Explain.

WEEK 15

Reading a Short Story For use with *Reader's Handbook* pages 294–314

Daily Lessons	Summary*
Lesson 1 **Characteristics of Short Stories**	Discuss with students the characteristics of short stories. Have students preview this section of the *Reader's Handbook*.
Lesson 2 **Preview and Plan to Read a Short Story**	Work with students to explore how they should preview and plan to read a short story.
Lesson 3 **Short Stories and Graphic Organizers**	Build an understanding of the various graphic organizers students can use as they read short stories.
Lesson 4 **Rereading Strategy: Close Reading**	Introduce students to the strategy of close reading. Work through the example of close reading with the class.

*Use these notes to help you teach a mini-lesson or to teach a briefer, shorter version of the lessons for more proficient students.

Lesson Resources

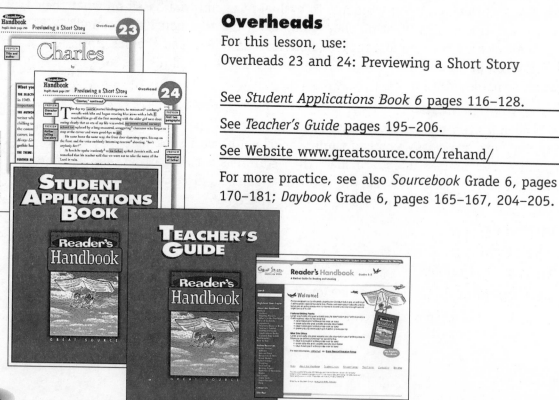

Overheads

For this lesson, use:
Overheads 23 and 24: Previewing a Short Story

See *Student Applications Book 6* pages 116–128.

See *Teacher's Guide* pages 195–206.

See Website www.greatsource.com/rehand/

For more practice, see also *Sourcebook* Grade 6, pages 170–181; *Daybook* Grade 6, pages 165–167, 204–205.

WEEK 16

Focus on Plot

For use with *Reader's Handbook* pages 368–375

Daily Lessons	Summary*
Lesson 1 **Parts of a Plot**	Work with students to identify the five main parts of a plot: the exposition, rising action, climax, falling action, and resolution.
Lesson 2 **Understanding Flashbacks**	Introduce the literary device of flashback. Discuss its purpose with students.
Lesson 3 **Understanding Subplots**	Work with students to explore the relationship between plots and subplots.
Lesson 4 **Plot and Graphic Organizers**	Review the various graphic organizers students can use **to** help them keep track of a story's action.

*Use these notes to help you teach a mini-lesson or to teach a briefer, shorter version of the lessons for more proficient students.

Lesson Resources

See *Student Applications Book 6* pages 148–149.

See *Teacher's Guide* pages 237–241.

See Website www.greatsource.com/rehand/

For more practice, see also *Sourcebook* Grade 6, pages 170–181; *Daybook* Grade 6, pages 165–167, 204–205.

WEEK 15
Lesson 1 Characteristics of Short Stories

For use with *Reader's Handbook* pages 294–314

Goals

In this lesson, students discuss the characteristics of short stories and preview this section of the *Reader's Handbook*.

Teaching Focus

Background

Before introducing this section of the handbook, it is beneficial to first activate students' prior knowledge about short stories and then give them the opportunity to preview the material on pages 294–314.

Instruction

Discuss with students what they know about short stories. Brainstorm characteristics of short stories with the class and create a Web for "short story." (For more information on Webs, see page 684 in the *Reader's Handbook*.) Explain that in this section of the handbook, students will learn more about short stories and how they can use the reading process to get the most out of this type of reading.

Teaching Approach

Use of the Handbook

Read aloud the introduction to the unit on page 294. Have students work in pairs to preview the section, excluding the sample short story (pages 296–303). Remind them to pay attention to headings, checklists, graphics, and boldface terms. Discuss what students learn from previewing. Ask students if they have anything to add to the Web now that they have previewed the section.

Extend the Handbook

Ask students to set a purpose and plan for reading this section by jotting down their thoughts in their journals. What questions do they have about this section of the *Reader's Handbook*? What do they hope to learn from reading about short stories?

For more practice, see pages 116–128 of the *Student Applications Book 6*.

Assessment

Ask students:

■ What are three characteristics of a short story?

■ What did you learn about this section by previewing it?

■ Was previewing the section helpful? Why or why not?

WEEK 15
Lesson 2

Preview and Plan to Read a Short Story

For use with *Reader's Handbook* pages 295–305

Goals

In this lesson, students learn ways of previewing and planning to read short stories.

Teaching Focus

Background

Throughout the *Reader's Handbook*, students are encouraged to apply the stages of the reading process to various genres. By previewing and planning to read "Charles," students review Before Reading steps introduced previously in lessons and modify them to a lesson on reading a short story.

Instruction

Review with students the Before Reading stages (pages 32–33). Explain that in this lesson they will use two of these strategies—preview and plan—before reading a short story. Discuss what students recall about previewing and planning to read a short story from their work in the previous lesson. Do students think previewing and planning will be different for a short story than for other genres they have learned about in the *Reader's Handbook*? Why or why not?

Teaching Approach

Use of the Handbook

Review with the class the Preview Checklist on page 295. Then either as a whole class or in small groups, have students use the checklist to preview the short story "Charles." Encourage students to pay attention to the annotations and highlighted information throughout the story. After previewing, have a student volunteer read aloud the top of page 304. Then read and discuss the three planning suggestions on pages 304–305.

Extend the Handbook

Have students create "previewing and planning" fact sheets to use the next time they read a short story. They might copy the Preview Checklist from page 295 or jot down other important previewing and planning facts they want to remember whenever they read short stories.

Assessment

Ask students:

■ What are three things to look for when you preview a short story?

■ Why is it helpful to preview and plan for reading a short story?

WEEK 15
Lesson 3 Short Stories and Graphic Organizers

For use with *Reader's Handbook* pages 306–308

Goals

In this lesson, students explore various graphic organizers they can use to help them keep track of information as they read short stories.

Teaching Focus

Background

There are a variety of graphic organizers readers can use to help them as they read a short story. Reading for enjoyment doesn't often necessitate the use of a graphic organizer, but reading assigned short stories, where a closer reading of the text may be required, does. Students will benefit from both an overview of the strategy of using graphic organizers and an understanding of when to use each.

Instruction

Discuss graphic organizers with students. You might ask them what they know about graphic organizers or what types of graphic organizers they have used. Point out that graphic organizers can be used with all kinds of reading materials to help readers keep track of important information. Explain that with short stories graphic organizers are often used to help readers focus on characters and plot.

Teaching Approach

Use of the Handbook

Read aloud the top of page 306 in the *Reader's Handbook*. Then divide the class into five groups. Assign each of the groups one of the graphic organizers on pages 306–308. Ask each group to "teach" the rest of the class how to use their graphic organizer. Remind groups to include the purpose for their graphic organizer.

Extend the Handbook

Have students use one of the graphic organizers they learned about in this lesson to help them keep track of information in a short story of their choice (they might look in a reading textbook for examples).

Assessment

Ask students:

■ How can the strategy of using graphic organizers help you when you read a short story?

■ How will you decide which graphic organizer to use?

WEEK 15
Lesson 4 — Rereading Strategy: Close Reading

For use with *Reader's Handbook* page 312

Goals

In this lesson, students explore close reading, a strategy designed to help readers reflect on and remember the details of what they've read.

Teaching Focus

Background
Close reading in this lesson involves rereading one short segment of a piece in greater detail, paying attention to every word. In close reading, readers rely on self-questioning and self-monitoring to make meaning of the text.

Instruction
Review with students the After Reading stage of the reading process. Explain that in this lesson they will learn about close reading, a rereading strategy that will help them deepen their understanding of the material.

Teaching Approach

Use of the Handbook
Read aloud or have a student volunteer read aloud the top of page 312. Discuss the information on close reading. Then work through the sample Double-entry Journal with the class. If students are having trouble understanding this strategy, walk them through another section of the story as you fill in a Double-entry Journal. For more information on close reading, see pages 642–643 in the *Reader's Handbook*.

Extend the Handbook
Have students return to the short story they used in Lesson 2. Ask them to create a Double-entry Journal for part of the story. Remind them to choose a part of the story that they feel is important to the story as a whole. Discuss students' thoughts on close reading after they complete the activity.

Assessment
Ask students:
■ What is close reading?

■ What is the purpose of close reading?

■ Did doing a close reading of "Charles" help you understand the story better? Explain.

WEEK 16
Lesson 1 — Parts of a Plot

For use with *Reader's Handbook* page 369

Goals

In this lesson, students examine the five main parts of a plot—the exposition, rising action, climax, falling action, and resolution.

Teaching Focus

Background

This unit focuses on key issues related to plot, including the use of subplots and flashbacks. In order to understand the complexities of plot and its structure, it is useful for students to first identify the five main parts of the plot and their function.

Instruction

Draw a sketch of a mountain on the board, similar to the one on page 369 of the *Reader's Handbook*. Explain to students that the action of a plot is often like that of climbing a mountain; the story begins, action increases up the mountain until it reaches the peak, and then it is downhill to the end of the story. Point out that there are specific terms for each part of the plot. Write the five parts of the plot next to the corresponding areas of the mountain (see page 369).

Teaching Approach

Use of the Handbook

Read aloud the top of page 369 of the *Reader's Handbook*. Then ask student volunteers to read aloud the description of the five parts of a plot. Review with the class the Plot Diagram. Explain that readers can use a Plot Diagram to keep track of action in a story.

Extend the Handbook

Have students work in pairs to create a Plot Diagram for a familiar story, such as a fairy tale. Can partners identify all five parts of the plot? Point out that not all stories follow this standard plot structure. If their story doesn't fit the standard diagram, challenge partners to create a custom Plot Diagram.

For more practice, see pages 148–149 of the *Student Applications Book 6*.

Assessment

Ask students:

■ What are the five parts of a plot?

■ How can you use your understanding of these parts of a plot to help you keep track of a story's action?

WEEK 16
Lesson 2 Understanding Flashbacks

For use with *Reader's Handbook* page 372

Goals

In this lesson, students learn what a flashback is and its role in the plot of a story.

Teaching Focus

Background

Proficient readers understand that authors use the literary device of flashback to provide us with important background information about current plot events. The ability to both recognize a flashback and understand its relationship to the current plot situation is critical in order for students to get the most out of their reading.

Instruction

Discuss with students the term *flashback*. What do students think it means? Can they use word analysis to guess its meaning? Explain that a flashback is a literary device that allows an author to present events that happened before the time of the current story. Discuss with students why they think authors would use flashbacks.

Teaching Approach

Use of the Handbook

Either as a whole class or in small groups, have students read the information on flashbacks on page 372 of the *Reader's Handbook*. Work with the whole class or groups to create a graphic organizer to use for identifying and keeping track of flashbacks.

Extend the Handbook

Have students work in small groups to develop examples of flashbacks. Rather than have them write a story, ask students to tell stories to each other that involve the use of flashback. After each story, have groups discuss the use of flashback and what information it provided. Ask groups how the stories would be different if the flashbacks were left out.

Assessment

Ask students:

■ What is a flashback?

■ What is the purpose of a flashback?

■ How can you identify a flashback in a story?

■ Do flashbacks enhance your enjoyment of stories? Explain.

WEEK 16
Lesson 3 Understanding Subplots

For use with *Reader's Handbook* page 373

Goals

In this lesson, students learn about subplots and their relationship to the central plot of a story.

Teaching Focus

Background

One of the key distinctions between short stories and novels is the use of subplots. Short stories typically revolve around one main plot. Novels, on the other hand, include the main plot plus one or more subplots. Identifying the subplots and separating them from the main plot will enhance students' understanding of the text.

Instruction

Explain to students that while most short stories focus on just one main plot, longer stories and novels often include the main plot plus one or more subplots. Discuss with students the difference between plot and subplot. Point out that subplots are still important to the story; they often relate to the main plot in some way and sometimes connect to the story's theme. Use examples from familiar novels to illustrate the relationship between plots and subplots.

Teaching Approach

Use of the Handbook

Read aloud or have student volunteers read aloud the first two paragraphs on page 373 of the *Reader's Handbook*. Then explore the plot and subplot illustration with the class. Be sure students understand the analogy between the satellites orbiting the planet and subplots "orbiting" the main plot in a story.

Extend the Handbook

Have students work in small groups to hold book discussions about a novel they have recently read. Ask groups to summarize the main plot, and then identify any subplots. Encourage groups to use a Story Organizer like the one on page 373 to help them keep track of the events in the subplot. After the groups identify the plot and subplot, encourage them to discuss the relationship between the two.

Assessment

Ask students:

■ What is a subplot? How do subplots relate to the main plot of a story?

■ How does identifying a subplot help you read stories?

WEEK 16
Lesson 4 Plot and Graphic Organizers

For use with *Reader's Handbook* pages 369–375

Goals

In this lesson, students review the various graphic organizers they can use to help them keep track of the plot of a story.

Teaching Focus

Background

One of the best ways to keep track of the plot, or action of a story, is to use graphic organizers. As discussed in previous lessons, Plot Diagrams, Story Organizers, and other organizers enable readers to identify key parts of the story.

Instruction

Review with students the three graphic organizers discussed in this unit—Plot Diagram, Storyboard, and Story Organizer. Ask students what the purpose of these organizers is. Lead students to recognize that graphic organizers can help them keep track of the story's action and separate key aspects of the plot from lesser details.

Teaching Approach

Use of the Handbook

Read aloud the information under "Using Graphic Organizers" on page 371 of the *Reader's Handbook*. Then work through the example of a Storyboard with the class. List the three graphic organizers (Plot Diagram, Storyboard, Story Organizer) from this unit and their characteristics on the board. Discuss with the class the differences between these organizers. Ask students how they can decide which tool to use.

Extend the Handbook

Invite students to choose one of their own fictional pieces to share with a partner. Have partners use a graphic organizer to help them keep track of the story's plot. Discuss with partners their choice of graphic organizers. Did creating the graphic organizer affect their understanding of the story? Why or why not?

For more practice, see pages 148–149 of the *Student Applications Book 6.*

Assessment

Ask students:

■ Which graphic organizer do you find helps you the most when reading fiction? Why?

■ What was the most important thing you learned from this unit on plot? Explain.

WEEK 17

Focus on Characters

For use with *Reader's Handbook* pages 340–350

Daily Lessons	Summary*
Lesson 1 **Focus on Characters:** **An Overview**	Review with students what they know about characters. Have them preview this section of the handbook.
Lesson 2 **Character-Related** **Terms**	Work with students to define the specialized terms used for analyzing characters in a story. Have students create mini-glossaries for these terms.
Lesson 3 **Analyzing Characters**	Help students identify graphic organizers that can be used to analyze characters. Explore the distinct features and purposes of each type of organizer.
Lesson 4 **Characters and Theme**	Build an understanding of the relationship between a story's characters and its theme. Discuss how what a character says, thinks, or does can offer clues about theme.

*Use these notes to help you teach a mini-lesson or to teach a briefer, shorter version of the lessons for more proficient students.

Lesson Resources

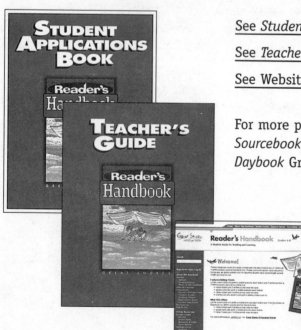

See *Student Applications Book 6* pages 141–143.

See *Teacher's Guide* pages 220–226.

See Website www.greatsource.com/rehand/

For more practice, see also *Sourcebook* Grade 6, page 50–57; *Daybook* Grade 6, pages 42–44.

WEEK 18

Focus on Setting

For use with *Reader's Handbook* pages 351–359

Daily Lessons	Summary*
Lesson 1 **Understanding Setting**	Have students examine the literary element of setting and the strategies they can use to analyze it.
Lesson 2 **Setting and Mood**	Work with students to explore the relationship between a story's setting and its mood.
Lesson 3 **Setting and Characters**	Help students recognize the relationship between a story's setting and its characters. Discuss how readers can make inferences about a character's personality based on how the character reacts to the setting.
Lesson 4 **Setting and Plot**	Discuss with students how changes in setting can signify changes in the story's action.

*Use these notes to help you teach a mini-lesson or to teach a briefer, shorter version of the lessons for more proficient students.

Lesson Resources

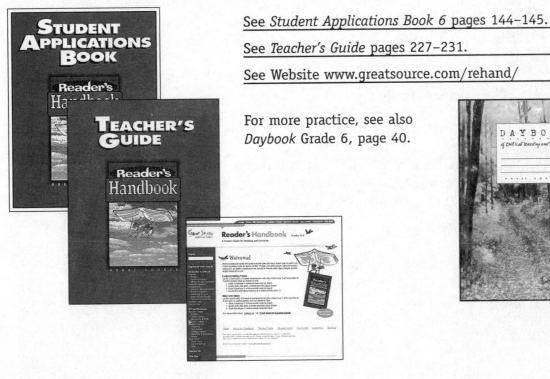

See *Student Applications Book 6* pages 144–145.

See *Teacher's Guide* pages 227–231.

See Website www.greatsource.com/rehand/

For more practice, see also *Daybook* Grade 6, page 40.

WEEK 17
Lesson 1 Focus on Characters: An Overview

For use with *Reader's Handbook* pages 340–350

Goals

In this lesson, students review what they know about characters and preview this section of the handbook.

Teaching Focus

Background

By sixth grade, students generally have at least a basic understanding of the story elements of character and characterization. This unit hopes to broaden students' understanding as they identify a variety of character types, look at graphic organizers that can be used to analyze characters, and explore the relationship between characters and theme. Activating students' prior knowledge of characters and allowing them to preview the section will help them take a more active part in the unit.

Instruction

Ask students what they know about *characters*. List their answers on the board. (Depending on the number and type of answers, you might organize them using a Concept Web or other organizers.) Explain that in this unit they will explore strategies readers can use to analyze characters and their relationship to other story elements.

Teaching Approach

Use of the Handbook

Read aloud the top of page 340 of the *Reader's Handbook*. Discuss with students the goals of the section. Then divide the class into small groups. Have groups preview the section on characters (pages 340–350). When groups are finished, discuss their preview. What did they notice about this unit?

Extend the Handbook

Ask students to reflect on their previews in their journals. As they reflect, ask them to consider questions such as these: What is my purpose for reading this unit? How well do I understand characterization?

For more practice, see pages 141–143 of the *Student Applications Book 6*.

Assessment

Ask students:

■ What did you learn from previewing this section on characters?

■ What questions do you have after previewing the material?

WEEK 17
Lesson 2 — Character-Related Terms

For use with *Reader's Handbook* pages 340–350

Goals

In this lesson, students examine the specialized terminology used when analyzing characters.

Teaching Focus

Background

In order to understand the information in this section, students need to familiarize themselves with the literary terminology used in it. A general understanding of terms such as *protagonist*, *antagonist*, and *dynamic character* will enable students to focus their attention on the reading material rather than on unfamiliar vocabulary.

Instruction

Ask student volunteers if they recall any boldface words from their preview of this section. List their responses on the board. Explain that this section contains a number of literary terms with which they may not be familiar. Point out that learning these terms will not only help them read about characterization, but it will also help them talk and write about characters more effectively.

Teaching Approach

Use of the Handbook

Have students work in pairs to create mini-glossaries of character-specific terminology. Ask partners to skim pages 340–350 and look for the following terms: *protagonist* (page 345), *main character* (page 340), *minor character* (page 340), *antagonist* (page 345), *static character* (page 348), and *dynamic character* (page 348). Point out that all these terms relate to ways of categorizing characters in a story. Ask pairs to write the terms and their definitions in their reading journals. Challenge pairs to define each term in their own words.

Extend the Handbook

Ask pairs to apply these terms to characters from a familiar fairy tale. Have students explain how they matched each character to the correct character type.

Assessment

Ask students:

■ What are three character-related terms you learned in this lesson? Define each.

■ How does categorizing characters help you understand them? Explain.

WEEK 17
Lesson 3 Analyzing Characters

For use with *Reader's Handbook* pages 343–350

Goals

In this lesson, students explore the various reading tools they can use to help them analyze characters.

Teaching Focus

Background

This section of the *Reader's Handbook* includes a number of useful reading tools for analyzing characters. The key to using them effectively is to understand the purpose of each. Recognizing what makes each tool distinctive will help students determine when to use them.

Instruction

Ask students to describe any of the reading tools they can recall from their preview of this section. Explain that there are four different reading tools discussed in this section: Character Map, Character Web, Inference Chart, and Character Development Chart. Point out that while all four of these can be used to analyze characters, each organizer each has a distinct purpose and features.

Teaching Approach

Use of the Handbook

Divide the class into four groups. Assign each group one of the following: Character Map (pages 341 and 343), Character Web (page 344), Inference Chart (page 347), Character Development Chart (page 350). Ask groups to explore their tool to find answers to the following questions: What are the features of this reading tool? Why would readers use it?

For more information on Character Development Charts, see page 668 of the *Reader's Handbook*; Character Map, page 668; Inference Chart, page 672, and Web, page 684.

Extend the Handbook

Have students choose one of the reading tools discussed in this lesson to help them understand a character in a familiar story. Remind them to choose their organizer based on their purpose.

Assessment

Ask students:

■ What reading tool would you use to keep track of how a character changes? Why?

■ How can reading tools help you analyze characters?

WEEK 17
Lesson 4 Characters and Theme

For use with *Reader's Handbook* pages 347–348

Goals

In this lesson, students explore the relationship between a story's characters and its theme.

Teaching Focus

Background

Proficient readers recognize that a character's words, thoughts, and actions can provide clues to the story's themes. In this lesson, students learn how a character's statements or thoughts about life can provide clues to theme. They also learn how changes in a character may signify an important theme.

Instruction

Explain to students that a theme is a general statement about life that readers construct from the story as they read. Point out that a theme is very rarely stated directly. Instead, readers need to look for clues to theme. Tell students that looking at what a character says, thinks, and does can give readers hints about theme.

Teaching Approach

Use of the Handbook

Read aloud the first few paragraphs on page 347 of the *Reader's Handbook*. Then read aloud the excerpt from *The Cay*. Think aloud as you read to show students how you develop ideas about theme based on what Timothy has to say. Then read aloud the top of page 348. Ask a student volunteer to read aloud the next excerpt from *The Cay*. Discuss how the change in Philip provides clues about a theme of the story.

For more information on theme, see pages 376–382 in the *Reader's Handbook*.

Extend the Handbook

Have students work in small groups to discuss other examples of how characters and theme interact. Prompt them to use what characters say, think, or do as clues to a story's theme. If the class has recently read a novel or short story, ask groups to first brainstorm possible themes for the story; then have them choose one and discuss the connection between the story characters and this theme.

Assessment

Ask students:

■ What is a theme?

■ How would you describe the relationship between a story's characters and its themes?

■ What part of this unit do you still have questions about? What can you do to better understand it?

WEEK 18
Lesson 1 Understanding Setting

For use with *Reader's Handbook* pages 351–353, 358–359

Goals

In this lesson, students learn how to determine the setting of a story and why this literary element is important.

Teaching Focus

Background
Setting is often an integral part of a story. The setting provides a context for the action of the story and helps readers visualize where the events of the story take place. It is the lens through which the story is seen.

Instruction
Discuss with students what they know about setting. List their responses on the board. Explain that every story has a setting, a time and place in which the story takes place. Point out that while some stories have very detailed, clear settings, other settings are subtler. Readers need to look for clues in the story, such as a specific date, historical period, or place name, to help them get a sense of when and where the story takes place. Discuss with students what types of clues authors might provide about setting. Talk also about how important a setting can be to a story and how it is much more than merely flowery descriptive language that surrounds the action of the story.

Teaching Approach

Use of the Handbook
Divide the class into small groups. Have each group read and discuss the information on pages 351–353. Ask groups to summarize their discussions and share them with the rest of the class. Then have students read pages 358–359 independently. Discuss the two After Reading ideas for understanding setting.

For more information on setting, see page 402 in the *Reader's Handbook*.

Extend the Handbook
Have students look for clues about setting in a story of their own choosing. Invite students to create setting Storyboards for their story, using the example on page 359 of the *Reader's Handbook*.

For more practice, see pages 144–145 of the *Student Applications Book 6*.

Assessment
Ask students:

■ What are three clues to look for to determine the setting of a story?

■ Why is it important to determine the setting of a story?

WEEK 18
Lesson 2 — Setting and Mood

For use with *Reader's Handbook* pages 354–355

Goals

In this lesson, students examine the relationship between a story's setting and its mood.

Teaching Focus

Background
One reason the setting of a fictional piece is important is that it often helps establish the mood, or atmosphere, of the piece. Mood can be a difficult literary concept for students to comprehend; examining it within the context of setting, a more familiar concept, can help students to grasp it more readily.

Instruction
Ask students what it means when someone tells them that they are in a bad mood. How would students describe mood? Explain that, like people, stories have moods, too. Point out that one way for readers to determine the mood, or feeling, of a story is by looking at setting. Discuss with students how they think the setting and mood of a story might be connected.

For more information on mood, see page 397 of the *Reader's Handbook*.

Teaching Approach

Use of the Handbook
Read aloud or have a student volunteer read aloud the top of page 354 of the *Reader's Handbook*. Then think aloud as you read the excerpt from *Shiloh* to the class. Focus your think-aloud on the excerpt's setting and mood. Then work with students to examine the example of the Double-entry Journal on page 355. Add to or modify the journal based on your think-aloud. Have students read and discuss the second excerpt from *Shiloh*. Do students agree that the description of setting creates a mood of fun and happiness?

Extend the Handbook
Have students return to the story they used in the previous lesson. Ask them to review the description of the setting and their Storyboards for clues about the mood of the story. Does the setting help establish the mood in this piece? Invite student volunteers to share their conclusions.

Assessment
Ask students:

■ How would you describe the connection between a story's setting and its mood?

■ What can you as a reader do to determine the mood of a story?

WEEK 18
Lesson 3 Setting and Characters

For use with *Reader's Handbook* page 356

Goals

In this lesson, students examine the relationship between a story's setting and its characters.

Teaching Focus

Background

Proficient readers understand that in order to truly understand a story's characters and their motivations, they must continually make inferences based on what each character says, thinks, and does. By paying attention to the setting and how a particular character responds to that setting, readers can infer information about the character's personality.

Instruction

Read aloud the following scenario to students: "It was a dark, gray night. The castle looked deserted. Lydia walked up the cracked stairs. She was scared but excited, too. This might be the answer, she thought, as she opened the front door." Ask students what they learned about Lydia from this scenario. Point out that from the description of the setting and how Lydia reacts to it, students can make inferences about Lydia's personality. Discuss students' thoughts about the relationship between setting and characters.

Teaching Approach

Use of the Handbook

Have students work in pairs to read and discuss the information on page 356 of the *Reader's Handbook*. Ask partners to create an Inference Chart for the excerpt on page 356. What can they tell about Shiloh from the author's description of the setting?

Extend the Handbook

Ask students to return to the story they have been using throughout this unit. Now have them focus on the clues they can get about characters based on how those characters react to the story's setting. Encourage students to jot down their thoughts about the relationship in their journals. Students might also reflect on how well they were able to make inferences during this activity. Did the setting provide enough clues? Have students explain.

Assessment

Ask students:

■ What can the setting of a story tell you about the story's characters?

■ What tools can help you keep track of the relationship between a story's setting and characters?

WEEK 18
Lesson 4 Setting and Plot

For use with *Reader's Handbook* page 357

Goals

In this lesson, students examine the connection between a story's setting and its plot.

Teaching Focus

Background

Just as setting can provide clues to a story's mood and its characters, it can also provide clues to a story's plot. In particular, changes in a story's setting often result in significant changes in the action of the story. In some stories, the setting itself can be part of the central conflict—for example, when the conflict revolves around "person vs. nature."

Instruction

Review with students the relationship between a story's setting and its characters and mood. Explain that a similar relationship exists between setting and plot, or the action of a story. What do students think that connection might be? Can they think of an example in which the setting or a change in the setting affects the action of a story? (You might spark their memories by mentioning familiar "person vs. nature" stories, such as *Hatchet* or *The Cay*.)

Teaching Approach

Use of the Handbook

Have students read the top of page 357 to themselves. Then read aloud the excerpt from *Shiloh*. Model a think aloud as you read, focusing on how the change in setting signals a change in the plot.

For more information on plot, see pages 400–401 of the *Reader's Handbook*.

Extend the Handbook

Have students return to the story they used in the previous lessons. Do students see any relationship between the setting and plot (specifically, changes in setting and changes in plot)? Now that students have examined how setting affects characters, mood, and plot, which of these relationships is most obvious in their story? Have students summarize their findings in their journals.

For more practice, see pages 144–145 and 148–149 of the *Student Applications Book 6*.

Assessment

Ask students:

■ How would you describe the relationship between setting and plot?

■ Has your understanding of setting changed after completing this unit? Explain.

Reading a Novel

For use with *Reader's Handbook* pages 315–339

Daily Lessons	Summary*
Lesson 1 **What Is a Novel?**	Discuss with the class what distinguishes novels from other forms of writing.
Lesson 2 **Get Set to Read**	Review with students the steps in the Before Reading stage of the reading process. Discuss the Setting a Purpose questions.
Lesson 3 **Preview a Novel**	Work with the class to examine the various features of a novel that can be used for previewing.
Lesson 4 **Read with a Purpose (Part 1)**	Students explore point of view, characters, setting, and plot as they relate to novels.

*Use these notes to help you teach a mini-lesson or to teach a briefer, shorter version of the lessons for more proficient students.

Lesson Resources

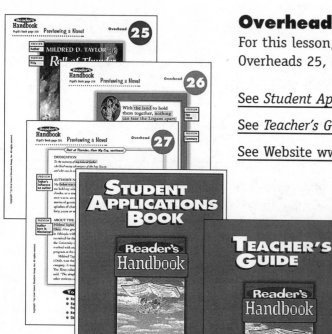

Overheads

For this lesson, use:
Overheads 25, 26, 27: Previewing a Novel

See *Student Applications Book 6* pages 129–140.

See *Teacher's Guide* pages 207–219.

See Website www.greatsource.com/rehand/

For more practice, see also *Sourcebook* Grade 6, pages 102–120, 182–189; *Daybook* Grade 6, pages 42–46, 66–67.

Reading a Novel (continued) For use with *Reader's Handbook* pages 315–339

Daily Lessons	Summary*
Lesson 5 **Read with a Purpose** **(Part 2)**	Review with students the last two questions from Setting a Purpose. Discuss ways to examine theme and author's style.
Lesson 6 **After Reading** **a Novel**	Work with students to identify specific ways to absorb what they read.
Lesson 7 **Rereading Strategy:** **Using Graphic Organizers**	Explore how and why to use graphic organizers when reading novels.
Lesson 8 **Reviewing the Novel**	Review the steps in the reading process and how to incorporate them when reading a novel.

*Use these notes to help you teach a mini-lesson or to teach a briefer, shorter version of the lessons for more proficient students.

Lesson Resources

Overheads

For this lesson, use:
Overheads 25, 26, 27: Previewing a Novel

See *Student Applications Book 6* pages 129–140.

See *Teacher's Guide* pages 207–219.

See Website www.greatsource.com/rehand/

For more practice, see also *Sourcebook* Grade 6, pages 102–121, 182–189; *Daybook* Grade 6, pages 42–46, 66–67.

WEEK 19
Lesson 1   What Is a Novel?

For use with *Reader's Handbook* pages 315–339

Goals

In this lesson, students learn what distinguishes a novel from other types of writing.

Teaching Focus

Background

By sixth grade, students have undoubtedly read and been exposed to numerous novels. Have they ever thought about what sets novels apart from other forms of writing? In this lesson, students will identify these characteristics to better appreciate what makes a novel a novel.

Instruction

Explain to students that they are about to begin a two-week unit on reading a novel. Ask student volunteers to list what they know about novels. (Students might offer ideas such as *work of fiction, chapters,* and *characters.*) Use the list to compare and contrast novels with other forms of fiction.

Teaching Approach

Use of the Handbook

Ask students to skim pages 315–339 in the handbook to get a sense of what this unit will cover. Then have student volunteers read aloud page 315. Discuss how the list of characteristics developed by the class corresponds to the characteristics mentioned in this introductory section.

Extend the Handbook

Invite students to list favorite novels they have read or that have been read to them. Have them choose one from their list to write about in their journals. Students might focus on why the book is a favorite or on any other aspect of the novel that was meaningful to them.

For additional practice, use pages 129–140 of the *Student Applications Book 6.*

Assessment

Ask students:

■ What are three characteristics of a novel?

■ How is a novel different from other forms of writing?

■ What do you like best about reading novels? Why?

WEEK 19
Lesson 2 Get Set to Read

For use with *Reader's Handbook* pages 316–321

Goals

In this lesson, students review the steps involved in the Before Reading stage and think about the importance of setting a purpose.

Teaching Focus

Background

Ask most adult readers why they choose to read a novel and they will tell you that a novel is enjoyable. It is exciting to get caught up in complex plots and characters. Because novels are long and complex, less proficient readers may get bogged down or overwhelmed when reading them. Setting a purpose before starting a novel will give students a focus for their reading and help them derive more meaning from the text.

Instruction

Ask students why they read novels. Answers might include: *I like them. They are fun to read. My teacher makes me.* Explain to students that most often readers choose to read novels for entertainment. Discuss with the class what makes reading a novel enjoyable. Lead students to recognize that in order to have fun reading, they must understand what they read. Explain that there are six main questions readers can ask themselves before reading a novel to help them better understand, and therefore better enjoy, what they read.

Teaching Approach

Use of the Handbook

Have students read page 316. Either as a whole class or in small groups, have students discuss the six questions that they can use to set a purpose for reading a novel. If students need a review of the Before Reading stage, have them reread the section on Before Reading on pages 32–33 of the *Reader's Handbook*.

Extend the Handbook

For additional practice in setting a purpose before reading a novel, have students complete pages 129–140 in the *Student Applications Book 6*.

Assessment

Ask students:

■ What are the six questions to ask yourself before reading a novel?

■ Which questions do you ask already? Which do you need to start asking?

■ How is a novel different from other forms of writing?

■ What do you like best about reading novels? Why?

WEEK 19
Lesson 3   Preview a Novel

For use with *Reader's Handbook* pages 317–320

Goals

In this lesson, students learn ways to preview a novel.

Teaching Focus

Background

Good readers preview a novel without even thinking about it. They look at the book jacket, skim the table of contents, and read the preface. All these techniques help them get a sense of what they are going to read and access prior knowledge. Unfortunately, not all readers take the time to do this before reading. This lesson will encourage students to preview and provide step-by-step models for doing so.

Instruction

Ask students what they do before going to see a new movie. Do they choose a movie based on commercials? Do they watch "previews" or hear about new films from friends? Explain that all these are ways of previewing. Readers do the same before they start to read. Book publishers invite readers to preview by providing certain standard elements, such as book jackets and cover illustrations. Can students think of other elements that they use for previewing?

Teaching Approach

Use of the Handbook

Read aloud page 317. Then break students into small groups, and have them note the different previewing features described in the model on pages 318–319. What do the groups learn about this novel from these features? Invite groups to continue previewing in the same fashion through page 320.

Extend the Handbook

Have students remain in their groups to practice previewing a novel. Provide them with copies of other novels. Remind groups to use the Preview Checklist on page 317.

For more practice, use pages 129–140 of the *Student Applications Book 6.*

Assessment

Ask students:

■ What are three ways to preview a novel?

■ What is the purpose of previewing a novel?

WEEK 19
Lesson 4
Read with a Purpose (Part 1)

For use with *Reader's Handbook* pages 322–332

Goals

In this lesson, students learn about setting purposes for reading by examining the following questions: Who is telling the story? Who are the main characters? Where and when does the story take place? What happens?

Teaching Focus

Background

Good readers pose the six Setting a Purpose questions (page 316 of the handbook) prior to reading. They begin to answer these questions as they read. While more experienced readers do this unconsciously, students will benefit from a more direct step-by-step modeling of the process.

Instruction

Review with students the first four Setting a Purpose questions. Explain that in this lesson they are going to start answering those questions. Invite student volunteers to tell what they know about point of view, characters, setting, and plot. List their responses on the board.

Teaching Approach

Use of the Handbook

Read aloud page 322. Then break the class into four groups. Assign each group one of the following elements: point of view (page 323), characters (pages 323–326), setting (pages 327–330), plot (pages 331–332). Have each group read and discuss the element they were assigned in the handbook. Then ask groups to summarize their reading for the class. As they do, encourage them to add to or modify the lists on the board generated earlier.

Extend the Handbook

Have students choose a novel they have recently read or had read to them. In their journals, invite students to jot down answers to the first four Before Reading questions as they relate to the novel.

Assessment

Ask students:

■ What is point of view? Why is it important to know the point of view of a story?

■ How can setting affect what happens in a novel?

■ What is one tool you can use to understand characters or plot?

WEEK 20
Lesson 5 Read with a Purpose (Part 2)

For use with *Reader's Handbook* pages 333–334

Goals

In this lesson, students continue to practice setting purposes by asking the following questions: What is the author's central idea or message? How does the author express his or her ideas?

Teaching Focus

Background

Theme and author's style are two of the more challenging elements of a novel. While features such as point of view, setting, characters, and plot can typically be found within the story, theme and author's style need a more careful analysis of the text and the meaning behind it. This lesson introduces these two elements. For a more detailed discussion of theme, see pages 376–382.

Instruction

Review with students the last two Setting a Purpose questions. Explain that the first question—What is the author's central idea or message?—can be answered by examining the themes of the novel. The second question—How does the author express his or her ideas?—can be answered by looking at the author's style.

Teaching Approach

Use of the Handbook

Since theme and author's style are quite complex elements, either work as a whole class or divide into two groups with an instructor leading each. Read aloud or have student volunteers read aloud page 333. Discuss the usefulness of the three-step process for determining a theme. Then read together page 334. Work with students to understand the Double-entry Journal and how it helps clarify the author's style.

Extend the Handbook

Have students reflect on the theme or author's style of a familiar novel. Encourage them to use the tools modeled in the lesson to explore these elements.

Assessment

Ask students:

■ What three steps can help readers identify a theme in a novel?

■ What question can you ask yourself when looking at an author's style?

WEEK 20
Lesson 6 After Reading a Novel

For use with *Reader's Handbook* pages 336–339

Goals

In this lesson, students learn specific ways to absorb what they've read.

Teaching Focus

Background

Proficient readers take the time to contemplate what they read. Pausing and reflecting after reading leads to greater understanding and retention of texts.

Instruction

Ask students what they do after reading a great novel. Do they shut the book and move on to something else? Or do they think about what they've read? Do they tell a friend about the novel? Explain that there are a number of ways to absorb what they've read. Review with the class the steps in the After Reading stage of the reading process: pause and reflect, reread, and remember. See pages 35–37 of the *Reader's Handbook* for a more detailed review of this stage.

Teaching Approach

Use of the Handbook

Have students work in pairs to read pages 336–339. Ask partners to summarize what they read by listing ways they can pause and reflect, reread, and remember. Have partners discuss which techniques they use already and which they need to practice.

Extend the Handbook

Have students choose one of the techniques they need to practice using more often. Encourage them to apply the technique to a novel they recently finished reading.

For more practice, use pages 129–140 in the *Student Applications Book 6*.

Assessment

Ask students:

■ What are two techniques you can use after reading a novel?

■ What do you hope to gain by using these techniques?

WEEK 20
Lesson 7 Novels and Graphic Organizers

For use with *Reader's Handbook* pages 321–339

Goals

In this lesson, students learn how to apply the strategy of using graphic organizers when rereading novels.

Teaching Focus

Background

Although graphic organizers are often associated with nonfiction reading, they are also wonderful tools for reading fiction. Granted, few of us utilize them when reading purely for enjoyment, but graphic organizers come in handy for assigned reading, when understanding and remembering information are crucial.

Instruction

Ask students what they can do to organize information when reading a novel. Lead them to see that techniques such as making a Plot Diagram, Timeline, or Fiction Organizer are all ways to organize information. Explain that they are going to look back over this unit to identify these and other graphic organizers they can use as they read novels.

Teaching Approach

Use of the Handbook

Break the class into four or five small groups. Have each group skim through the unit for examples of graphic organizers. Ask groups to list the graphic organizers and their uses on a large piece of paper. As a whole class, have groups compare their lists and discuss which organizers they are familiar with and which they haven't used before.

Extend the Handbook

Have students choose one of the graphic organizers that they haven't used before. Encourage them to use it to organize information from a novel they have recently read.

Assessment

Ask students:

■ How can graphic organizers help when you reread a novel?

■ What are two graphic organizers you can use to help you organize information when reading a novel?

142

Reviewing the Novel

WEEK 20 Lesson 8

For use with *Reader's Handbook* pages 315–339

Goals

In this lesson, students review what they have learned and how to apply the reading process to novels.

Teaching Focus

Background

The first seven lessons in the unit focused on different ways to get more out of reading a novel. This lesson allows students to reflect on what they've learned and to develop a plan for applying what they've learned in the *Reader's Handbook* to other reading situations.

Instruction

Review with students what they've learned in this unit. You might create a chart on the board that lists the lessons and a brief summary of each (similar to the one on page 37 of the handbook). Discuss the steps involved in the reading process and how students can apply them when reading a novel.

Teaching Approach

Use of the Handbook

Have students review the information on pages 315–339 of the handbook. Encourage them to pay particular attention to parts of the unit that they still have questions about. To help them recognize which parts are difficult for them, ask students to choose the section of the unit that they feel they understand the most and the section they think they understand the least.

Extend the Handbook

Have students write a plan for how they will use the reading process the next time they read a novel. Invite volunteers to share their plans with the class.

Assessment

Ask students:

■ What are the steps in the process of reading a novel?

■ What are two strategies you can use when reading a novel?

■ How will you use this unit to help you become a better reader?

WEEK 21

Elements of Fiction

For use with *Reader's Handbook* pages 389–396

Daily Lessons	Summary*
Lesson 1 **Antagonist and Protagonist**	Discuss with students the literary elements of antagonist and protagonist and their relationship to one another. Brainstorm with students famous antagonist/protagonist pairs in literature and film.
Lesson 2 **Author's Purpose**	Students examine author's purpose in order to enhance their understanding of texts.
Lesson 3 **Dialogue and Dialect**	Help students understand the use of dialogue and dialect in literature. Have students rewrite a short piece without using dialogue.
Lesson 4 **Genre**	Build an understanding of the various genres found in fiction. Discuss the characteristics of different genres.

*Use these notes to help you teach a mini-lesson or to teach a briefer, shorter version of the lessons for more proficient students.

Lesson Resources

See *Teacher's Guide* pages 252–263.

See Website www.greatsource.com/rehand/

For more practice, see also *Daybook* Grade 6, pages 22–23, 26–31.

WEEK 22

Elements of Fiction (continued)

For use with *Reader's Handbook* pages 398–405

Daily Lessons	Summary*
Lesson 5 **Point of View**	Build an understanding of point of view and its effect on a story. Have students rewrite a short piece by changing its point of view.
Lesson 6 **Style**	Discuss the role author's style plays on readers' understanding and enjoyment of a story. Discuss the styles of popular authors, such as Gary Paulsen and Betsy Byars.
Lesson 7 **Symbol**	Help students understand the use of symbols in literary works. Have them identify symbols of their own.
Lesson 8 **Theme**	Discuss theme and its importance in literature. Have students explore themes of familiar stories and movies.

*Use these notes to help you teach a mini-lesson or to teach a briefer, shorter version of the lessons for more proficient students.

Lesson Resources

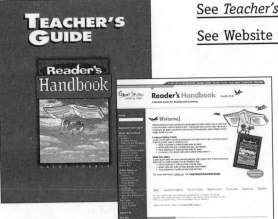

See *Teacher's Guide* pages 252–263.

See Website www.greatsource.com/rehand/

For more practice, see also *Daybook* Grade 6, pages 22–23, 26–31.

WEEK 21
Lesson 1 ▸ Antagonist and Protagonist

For use with *Reader's Handbook* page 390

Goals

In this lesson, students discuss the literary elements of protagonist and antagonist and examine their relationship to one another.

Teaching Focus

Background

The terms *protagonist* and *antagonist* were introduced in Week 17, Lesson 2. This lesson explores these concepts and their relationship to one another in more depth. Understanding the roles of the protagonist and antagonist will also lead to a deeper understanding of the central conflict in fictional works.

Instruction

Review the terms *protagonist* and *antagonist* with students. Explain that in works of fiction, the heart of the story often revolves around the relationship or conflict between the protagonist and the antagonist. Point out that neither the protagonist nor the antagonist needs to be human. Animals, forces of nature, even conflicts within a character can play these roles.

Teaching Approach

Use of the Handbook

Read aloud the first paragraph on page 390 of the *Reader's Handbook*. Then work through the excerpt with the class, pointing out the protagonist and antagonist as you proceed. Have students read the rest of the page independently. Discuss the description and definitions of protagonist and antagonist.

Extend the Handbook

Hold a class brainstorming session to come up with a list of famous antagonist/protagonist pairs from literature and film. (For example, Luke Skywalker and Darth Vader, Dorothy and the Wicked Witch, or the Three Little Pigs and the Big Bad Wolf.) Ask students to choose one pair from the list and write a brief explanation of the relationship between the two. Questions they might consider: What is the conflict between the two characters? Is this conflict a central part of the story's action?

Assessment

Ask students:

■ What is the relationship between a story's protagonist and its antagonist?

■ Why is it important to pay attention to this relationship?

WEEK 21
Lesson 2 Author's Purpose

For use with *Reader's Handbook* page 391

Goals

In this lesson, students determine author's purpose in order to better understand and evaluate what they read.

Teaching Focus

Background

Strong readers understand that authors have various reasons for writing. Even authors of fictional material often have purposes beyond entertainment; fiction can be used to enlighten or reveal an important truth. Recognizing the author's purpose enhances understanding of the text and its meaning.

Instruction

Ask students why they write: What is their purpose? List their responses on the board. Explain that authors also have reasons for writing. Use students' responses as a springboard for a discussion of author's purposes. Lead students to see that there are four basic purposes for writing: to explain or inform, to entertain, to persuade, or to enlighten or reveal an important truth.

Teaching Approach

Use of the Handbook

Work through the information on page 391 with the class. Discuss the description and definition of author's purpose. Remind students that many times the author's purpose will not be directly stated; rather, the reader has to infer the purpose. Discuss why determining the author's purpose will help students get more out of their reading.

Extend the Handbook

As a class, brainstorm a list of genres (for example, newspaper articles, editorials, mysteries, poetry). Work with the class to classify each genre under one or more of the four author's purposes. Explain that often the type of writing an author chooses is a clue to the author's purpose (for example, editorials are written to persuade and newspaper articles to inform).

Assessment

Ask students:

■ What are the four basic reasons, or purposes, an author might have for writing?

■ How does recognizing the author's purpose help you as a reader?

WEEK 21
Lesson 3 — Dialogue and Dialect

For use with *Reader's Handbook* pages 394–395

Goals

In this lesson, students explore dialogue and dialect and examine what each adds to fictional material.

Teaching Focus

Background

Proficient readers recognize that authors often rely on dialogue to reveal important information about their characters' personalities and motivations. Dialect, too, provides clues about characters and adds richness and realism to a story. Students will benefit from a close examination of these two literary devices.

Instruction

Ask student volunteers to define *dialogue*. If necessary, prompt students to define dialogue as "the words characters say." Discuss the importance of dialogue. Why do students think authors use it? Why do students use it in their own writing? Then provide some background on dialect. Discuss the different forms of language spoken between students and their peers or students and their parents. Students might brainstorm a list of words specific to their "dialect."

Teaching Approach

Use of the Handbook

Read aloud the first paragraph on page 394. Then act as narrator as two student volunteers read aloud the dialogue between Tom and Becky in the excerpt from *The Adventures of Tom Sawyer*. Note the rules for punctuating dialogue on the top of page 395. Then have a student volunteer read aloud the information on dialect. Return to the excerpt and focus on Twain's use of dialect. Discuss with students what dialect adds to the excerpt.

Extend the Handbook

To illustrate the importance of dialogue in a story, have students work in pairs to rewrite a short excerpt from a dialogue-rich story by taking out all the dialogue and replacing it with straight narration. Ask partners to compare the two versions. What happens to the piece when the dialogue is removed? Have pairs share their conclusions with the class.

Assessment

Ask students:

■ How would you define dialogue and dialect?

■ What do dialogue and dialect add to stories?

WEEK 21
Lesson 4 ▶ Genre

For use with *Reader's Handbook* page 396

Goals

In this lesson, students explore the various genres found in fiction and examine the characteristics of each genre.

Teaching Focus

Background

As readers, we make connections not only to the content of what we read but also to the literary genre in which it is presented. Understanding the specific characteristics and conventions associated with each genre provides background knowledge and helps us better comprehend the text.

Instruction

Brainstorm with the class different types of fiction, such as folktales, fairy tales, and fantasy. Explain that these categories are called genres and that each genre has certain characteristics. Ask students how they know when they are reading a fairy tale rather than a mystery. Explain that certain features, such as beginning a story with "Once upon a time," provide clues to the genre. Discuss how identifying the genre can help students as they read.

Teaching Approach

Use of the Handbook

Read aloud the first two paragraphs on the top of page 396 of the *Reader's Handbook*. Then work through the genre chart with students. Have students add to the chart by listing other familiar genres, such as science fiction, mystery, drama, and historical fiction, along with each genre's characteristics. Explain that there might be other features besides character, plot, setting, and theme that set these genres apart. Have students add columns to the chart as necessary.

Extend the Handbook

Ask each student to identify three favorite pieces of literature. Use their responses to create a graphic, such as a bar graph, to document the different genres represented. Does one genre dominate the graph? What do the results say about students' favorite genre choices? Discuss the results with the class.

Assessment

Ask students:

■ What is a genre?

■ How can knowing the genre help you when you read a piece of fiction?

WEEK 22
Lesson 5   Point of View

For use with *Reader's Handbook* pages 398–399

Goals

In this lesson, students explore point of view and how it affects a story.

Teaching Focus

Background

Proficient readers understand that the point of view of a story affects what information we receive. Recognizing the advantages as well as the limitations of the most common points of view—first-person, third-person limited, third-person omniscient—will enable students to read more critically.

Instruction

Write the following sentences on the board: *1. My heart pounded as I opened the door. Jeff watched in silence. Why wasn't he helping? I wondered. 2. Her heart pounded as she opened the door. Jeff watched in silence. 3. Her heart pounded as she opened the door. Jeff watched in silence, too frightened to move.* Discuss with the class the differences among the three scenarios. Explain that what changed was the point of view from which the scene was presented.

Teaching Approach

Use of the Handbook

Have students work in small groups to read and discuss pages 398–399 of the *Reader's Handbook*. After reading, come together as a class and return to the three scenarios discussed above. Ask student volunteers to identify the point of view of each. Talk about how changes in point of view alter the information available to the reader.

Extend the Handbook

Ask students to work in pairs to change the point of view of a familiar story or fairy tale (Jon Scieszka's *The True Story of the Three Little Pigs* is an excellent example). For shorter pieces, pairs might rework the entire piece; for longer pieces, have pairs choose a key excerpt to rewrite. Invite partners to share their rewrites with the class. Discuss how altering the point of view changes the story.

Assessment

Ask students:

■ What are the three most common points of view?

■ Why is it important to be aware of point of view when reading fiction?

WEEK 22
Lesson 6 Style

For use with *Reader's Handbook* page 403

Goals

In this lesson, students examine the role author's style plays in readers' understanding and enjoyment of a story.

Teaching Focus

Background
Evaluating an author's style can be tricky for students, especially since many of the differences in authors' styles are subtle ones. But recognizing characteristics of an author's style is critical for effectively evaluating fiction. Examining the three components of author's style will encourage students to focus their attention on this literary element as they read.

Instruction
Discuss with students what they think of when they hear the word *style*. How do they define it? What does it mean when someone talks about their "own style"? Explain that just as students themselves have distinctive styles, perhaps in the way they dress or the way they talk, authors have their own styles of writing. Explain that some writers use "big" words and sophisticated sentence structure; others are known for their short, to-the-point writing. Discuss with students why they think an author's style matters to the reader.

Teaching Approach

Use of the Handbook
Since style can be difficult for students to identify, work as a whole class to read and discuss the information on page 403 of the *Reader's Handbook*. Pay particular attention to the model. Discuss the call-outs and what they say about Louis Sachar's style.

Extend the Handbook
Gather examples of works by authors with particularly distinctive styles for students to examine. (Good choices include Gary Paulsen, Betsy Byars, and Byrd Baylor.) Have students meet in small groups to talk about the author's style. Questions for groups to consider: How would you describe the author's style? What effect does the style have on the story? How would the story be different if it were written in a different style?

Assessment
Ask students:
■ What are the three elements of author's style?

■ Why is it important to recognize and think about author's style?

WEEK 22
Lesson 7 Symbol

For use with *Reader's Handbook* page 404

Goals

In this lesson, students explore the use of symbols in literary works.

Teaching Focus

Background

As with style, the use of symbols can be difficult for students to grasp initially. Symbols embody ideas; identifying them demands a higher level of thinking than other more concrete kinds of literary elements. But understanding the use of symbols is important, particularly since symbols are often used to articulate a story's theme.

Instruction

Gather images of universal symbols, such as a heart, a dove, a stop sign, and a skull and crossbones. Display the images to the class. Discuss with students what each means. Explain that each of these concrete items is also a symbol—they represent something more than themselves. Point out that authors sometimes use symbols in their writing.

Teaching Approach

Use of the Handbook

Walk the class through the information on page 404 of the *Reader's Handbook*. Think aloud as you read the excerpt from *The Fragile Flag*. Model for students how you use the information from the text to determine what the flag represents. Explain that some symbols, like the stop sign, have a universal meaning that everyone agrees upon. But authors often use invested symbols, symbols that gain meaning based on how the author uses them in the context of the story. Discuss with students strategies for identifying invested symbols.

Extend the Handbook

Have students identify invested symbols of their own. Ask them to think about people, places, things, or events in their lives that mean something more than what they mean to others. For example, some students might consider their dog or cat a symbol for unconditional love or a soccer ball a symbol of achievement. Encourage students to reflect on the symbol and its meaning in their journals.

Assessment

Ask students:

■ What is the difference between a universal and an invested symbol?

■ Why do you think authors use symbols when they write?

152

WEEK 22
Lesson 8 — Theme

For use with *Reader's Handbook* page 405

Goals

In this lesson, students examine theme and its importance in literature.

Teaching Focus

Background

Of the five main story elements—characters, setting, plot, point of view, and theme—theme is one of the most complex or difficult to understand. But recognizing theme is also one of the most crucial steps for true understanding of a piece of fiction. Themes can be ambiguous; what one reader sees as a theme might be quite different from what another reader sees. Readers must be able to support their choice with evidence from the text. Direct instruction on strategies for determining theme will provide students with the tools necessary for inferring theme.

Instruction

Explain to students that a theme is a general statement about life that readers construct from the text as they read a story. Point out that a theme is very rarely stated directly. Instead, readers need to look for clues to theme. Review with students techniques for inferencing.

Teaching Approach

Use of the Handbook

Think aloud as you read the short excerpt from "Eleven." Focus your think-aloud on ways you can infer a theme of the story, including reflecting on the story's title. Point out that titles often provide clues to a story's theme. Then work through the information on the rest of page 405. Discuss the concept of theme with students. Encourage students to identify specific activities they can use for identifying theme, such as reflecting on the title, looking for how characters change, or asking themselves, "What is the meaning of the story?"

For more information on theme, see pages 376–382 in the *Reader's Handbook*.

Extend the Handbook

Ask students to work in small groups to discuss themes from familiar stories and movies, such as *The Wizard of Oz*. To help them identify theme, have groups use a Topic and Theme Organizer (see example on page 681 of the *Reader's Handbook*).

Assessment

Ask students:

■ What clues can you use to help identify theme?

■ How does determining the theme affect your understanding of a story?

WEEK 23

Reading a Poem

For use with *Reader's Handbook* pages 408–421

Daily Lessons	Summary*
Lesson 1 **Before Reading a Poem**	Review with students the Before Reading stage of the reading process. Explore how to apply these steps to reading poetry.
Lesson 2 **While Reading a Poem**	Work with students to explore ways to apply During Reading steps to reading a poem.
Lesson 3 **Reading Strategy: Close Reading**	Review the strategy of close reading. Help students as they apply it to reading a poem.
Lesson 4 **After Reading a Poem**	Help students apply the After Reading stage of the reading process to poetry. Build an understanding of the importance of paraphrasing a poem.

*Use these notes to help you teach a mini-lesson or to teach a briefer, shorter version of the lessons for more proficient students.

Lesson Resources

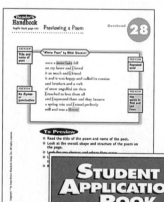

Overheads
For this lesson, use:
Overhead 28: Previewing a Poem

See *Student Applications Book 6* pages 154–164.

See *Teacher's Guide* pages 265–275.

See Website www.greatsource.com/rehand/

For more practice, see also *Daybook* Grade 6, pages 76–77, 181–182.

154

Elements of Poetry

For use with *Reader's Handbook* pages 446–464

Daily Lessons	Summary*
Lesson 1 **Forms of Poetry**	Build an understanding of lyric and narrative poetry. Have students use these categories to classify poems.
Lesson 2 **Figurative Language**	Work with students to explore figurative language, alliteration, metaphor, simile, personification, and onomatopoeia.
Lesson 3 **Playing with Words: Exaggeration and Idioms**	Help students understand the characteristics of exaggerations and idioms and what they add to a poem. Work with students to find examples of these devices in poetry.
Lesson 4 **Rhyme, Rhythm, and Repetition**	Discuss with students the use of rhyme, rhythm, and repetition in poetry. Have students identify the rhyme scheme in poems.

*Use these notes to help you teach a mini-lesson or to teach a briefer, shorter version of the lessons for more proficient students.

Lesson Resources

See *Teacher's Guide* pages 291–307.

See Website www.greatsource.com/rehand/

For more practice, see also *Daybook* Grade 6, pages 76–77, 181–182.

WEEK 23
Lesson 1 ▶ Before Reading a Poem

For use with *Reader's Handbook* pages 408–411

Goals

In this lesson, students explore Before Reading steps they can use to help them get ready to read a poem.

Teaching Focus

Background

There are few genres more well suited to the reading process than poetry. Poetry, with its imagery and metaphors, demands questioning, inferring, and thoughtful reflection. This unit provides suggestions for adapting the reading process and its strategies to reading poems.

Instruction

Review the Before Reading stage of the reading process. Remind students of the three Before Reading steps—Set a Purpose, Preview, and Plan. Explain that these steps can be used to help students prepare for reading poetry, as well as fiction and nonfiction. Discuss the benefits of taking the time before reading to set a purpose, preview, and plan.

Teaching Approach

Use of the Handbook

Read aloud or have a student volunteer read aloud the unit opener on page 408 of the *Reader's Handbook*. Work with students to set purposes for reading. Then divide the class into small groups to work through the preview and plan activities on pages 409–411. Come together as a whole class and discuss the four parts of the reading plan (page 411).

Extend the Handbook

Gather a variety of poems for students to explore (for example, *Near the Window Tree: Poems and Notes* by Karla Kuskin and "Neighborhood Odes" by Gary Soto). Invite students to choose a poem or two to explore throughout this unit. Ask students to apply the Before Reading steps discussed in this lesson to the poem. Encourage students to reflect on this activity in their journals.

For more practice, see pages 154–164 of the *Student Applications Book 6*.

Assessment

Ask students:

■ How can you apply the Before Reading steps of the reading process to poetry?

■ What is the purpose of applying these steps to poetry?

■ What is one useful strategy for reading poetry?

156

WEEK 23
Lesson 2   While Reading a Poem

For use with *Reader's Handbook* pages 413–418

Goals

In this lesson, students examine techniques for applying During Reading stages to poetry.

Teaching Focus

Background

A poem requires more than one reading in order to unlock its meaning. Reading with a purpose and making connections to the poetry will enable students to read with deeper understanding and enjoyment.

Instruction

Ask student volunteers to describe what they do when they read a poem. Explain that as they learned in the previous lesson, true understanding of poems usually requires numerous readings. Review the During Reading stage of the reading process (see pages 34–35 of the *Reader's Handbook* for more information). Point out that applying these steps while reading a poem will help students get the most out of their reading.

Teaching Approach

Use of the Handbook

Review the reading plan discussed in the previous lesson. Then walk students through the four approaches to reading poetry (pages 413–417). Discuss how each rereading adds layers of meaning to the poem. Spend time talking about how poems can be organized. End by asking students to read page 418 independently. Encourage them to make their own connections to "Winter Poem."

Extend the Handbook

Have students apply During Reading steps to the poem they chose in the previous lesson. Encourage them to create Double-entry Journals for each rereading, such as those on pages 413, 414, 415, and 417 of the *Reader's Handbook*. Either on sticky notes or in their journals, ask students to jot down any connections they make to the poem.

For more practice, see pages 154–164 of the *Student Applications Book 6*.

Assessment

Ask students:

■ Why is it important to read a poem more than once?

■ How will you use what you learned in this lesson the next time you read a poem?

WEEK 23
Lesson 3
Reading Strategy: Close Reading

For use with *Reader's Handbook* page 412

Goals

In this lesson, students review the strategy of close reading and apply it to reading poetry.

Teaching Focus

Background

Students were first introduced to the strategy of close reading in Week 15, Lesson 4. Here they will learn how to apply this strategy to reading poetry. Poems tend to be shorter than other forms of fiction, and each word carries a lot of weight. For this reason, close reading is a particularly useful strategy for poetry.

Instruction

Review with students the strategy of close reading. Remind students that close reading involves going word by word and line by line through a text. Discuss why students think this strategy might be helpful when reading a poem.

Teaching Approach

Use of the Handbook

Have a student volunteer read aloud the first paragraph on page 412 of the *Reader's Handbook*. Then walk students through the information on creating a Double-entry Journal. As a class, fill in the Double-entry Journal for "Winter Poem." Discuss how Double-entry Journals can help students perform a close reading of a poem.
For more information on Double-entry Journals, see page 671 of the *Reader's Handbook*.

Extend the Handbook

Ask students to return to the poem they have been using throughout this unit. Have students concentrate on a close reading of the poem. Encourage them to create Double-entry Journals, such as the one shown on page 412 of the handbook. As a class, discuss the benefits of close reading.

For more practice, see pages 154–164 of the *Student Applications Book 6*.

Assessment

Ask students:

■ What is close reading?

■ How does close reading affect your understanding of a poem?

■ What do you find most difficult about close reading? What can you do to make it easier?

WEEK 23
Lesson 4 After Reading a Poem

For use with *Reader's Handbook* pages 419–421

Goals

In this lesson, students review the After Reading stage of the reading process and apply it as a rereading strategy to poetry.

Teaching Focus

Background

Proficient readers recognize that taking the time after reading a poem to reflect and reread enhances their understanding and enjoyment of the material. Too often, students rush past this stage of the reading process. A step-by-step plan detailing key After Reading steps will encourage students to continue to think through the poem and its meaning once they have finished reading it.

Instruction

Review the After Reading stage of the reading process with students. (See pages 35–37 of the *Reader's Handbook* for more information.) Ask student volunteers to describe ways they might apply After Reading steps to a poem. How do students think these stages will help them understand poetry?

Teaching Approach

Use of the Handbook

Read aloud the top of page 419 of the *Reader's Handbook*. Walk students through the rereading checklist, and then continue reading this page. Work with students to understand the strategy of paraphrasing (page 420). Discuss how paraphrasing can enhance students' understanding of a poem. Then ask students to read the rest of page 420 and page 421 independently.

Extend the Handbook

Have students apply the strategy of paraphrasing to the poem they have been using throughout the unit. Encourage them to create Paraphrasing Charts, such as the one shown on page 420 of the handbook. Then ask students to paraphrase their poem to a partner.

For more practice, see pages 154–164 of the *Student Applications Book 6.*

Assessment

Ask students:

■ What strategies can you use after reading a poem to help you understand it?

■ What is the purpose of paraphrasing a poem?

WEEK 24
Lesson 1 ▸ Forms of Poetry

For use with *Reader's Handbook* pages 454 and 457

Goals

In this lesson, students explore lyric poetry and narrative poetry.

Teaching Focus

Background

Poems come in many varieties, from haiku to ballads. This lesson introduces students to two common forms—lyric and narrative poetry. Different types of poems require different focuses on the reader's part. Understanding the characteristics of lyric and narrative poetry will help students determine what strategies to use as they read each.

Instruction

Explain to students that in this lesson they will learn about two types of poetry—lyric and narrative. Ask student volunteers what they know about narrative poetry and lyric poetry. What do students predict might be characteristics of each? List their predictions on the board. Point out that once students know the characteristics of each type of poem, they will have a framework for reading and understanding them.

Teaching Approach

Use of the Handbook

Divide the class into four groups. Have two groups read about lyric poetry on page 454 of the handbook and two groups read about narrative poetry on page 457. Ask groups to summarize the material. Then ask the two groups who learned about lyric poetry to get together to plan a presentation on lyric poems. Ask the other two groups to do the same for narrative poems. After presentations, return to students' initial predictions. Modify them as necessary based on students' new understanding of lyric and narrative poetry.

Extend the Handbook

Have students gather in groups of four or five. Ask groups to share the poem they have been using throughout this unit. Would students classify the poems as lyric, narrative, or neither? Encourage students to tally and discuss the results. Questions to consider: Which type of poem was more common? How does the type of poem affect how students read it? Which type of poem do students enjoy more?

Assessment

Ask students:

■ What is the difference between lyric and narrative poetry?

■ How can classifying a poem help you as you read it?

WEEK 24
Lesson 2 — Figurative Language

For use with *Reader's Handbook* pages 447, 450, 455, 458, 459, and 464

Goals

In this lesson, students examine figurative language, including alliteration, metaphor, onomatopoeia, personification, and simile.

Teaching Focus

Background

Figurative language is a key component of poetry. Poets need to say what they want to say with few words. Therefore, their choice of words becomes extremely important. Recognizing the different types of figurative language and how poets use them to convey meaning will enhance students' appreciation of poems.

Instruction

Ask student volunteers to describe what they picture when they hear this phrase: *Her eyes were as green as emeralds.* Explain that this is an example of figurative language. Point out that poets use figurative language as a sort of shorthand— a way of creating vivid images in limited space. Explain that in this lesson, students will learn about five kinds of figurative language: alliteration, metaphor, onomatopoeia, personification, and simile.

Teaching Approach

Use of the Handbook

Read aloud page 450 of the *Reader's Handbook*. Then divide students into four groups. Assign each group one of the following: alliteration (page 447), metaphor and simile (pages 455 and 464), onomatopoeia (page 458), and personification (page 459). As they did in the previous lesson, have groups summarize and present one of the figures of speech to the class.

Extend the Handbook

Have students return to their chosen poem. This time, ask them to concentrate on the poet's use of figurative language. Encourage students to identify examples of figurative speech. Then have students reflect on the poet's use of figurative speech in their journals. Questions they might consider: What types of figurative speech does the poet use? What images do the examples suggest?

Assessment

Ask students:

■ What are five forms of figurative language? Define each.

■ How does recognizing figurative language affect your understanding and appreciation of a poem?

WEEK 24
Lesson 3

Playing with Words: Exaggeration and Idioms

For use with *Reader's Handbook* pages 449 and 452

Goals

In this lesson, students explore poets' use of exaggeration and idioms and what they add to a poem.

Teaching Focus

Background

Part of the fun of poetry can stem from the playfulness with which poets present their ideas. A large part of that playfulness comes through the poet's word choices. As discussed in the previous lesson, figurative speech is one way poets bring their poems to life. This lesson focuses on two more ways of "playing" with words—the use of exaggeration and idioms.

Instruction

Ask student volunteers to explain what the phrase "don't lose your cool" means. Discuss how the literal meaning of this phrase is very different from its common meaning. Explain that phrases such as this are called *idioms*. Then ask another student volunteer to use an example of exaggeration. Explain that exaggerations in poetry are another form of word play. Discuss why poets might use word play in their poems.

Teaching Approach

Use of the Handbook

Have students work in pairs to read and discuss the information on exaggeration (page 449) and idioms (page 452) in the *Reader's Handbook*. Come together as a class and have partners share what they learned. Discuss how exaggerations and idioms enhance readers' enjoyment of poetry.

Extend the Handbook

Have students work in small groups to find examples of exaggeration and idioms in other poems. They might use the poem they have worked on throughout the unit or examine other poems used in this section of the handbook. Ask groups to discuss why the poets might have chosen to use these particular phrases. What images do they suggest? How do the images connect to the poem's meaning?

Assessment

Ask students:

■ What is an idiom?

■ What do idioms and exaggeration add to poetry?

162

WEEK 24
Lesson 4
Rhyme, Rhythm, and Repetition

For use with *Reader's Handbook* pages 460–463

Goals

In this lesson, students examine the use of rhyme, rhythm, and repetition in poetry.

Teaching Focus

Background

Students are undoubtedly familiar with the concept of end rhymes; they have been hearing them since their nursery rhyme days. But concepts such as *internal rhyme*, *repetition*, and *rhythm* might be less familiar to them. An examination of these concepts and a discussion of their significance will enhance students' understanding and enjoyment of poetry.

Instruction

Ask student volunteers to repeat familiar nursery rhymes, such as "Hickory Dickory Dock" or "Twinkle Twinkle Little Star." Discuss what they notice about the use of rhyme in the verses. Explain that these are examples of end rhyme, or a repetition of sounds at the end of lines. Introduce the terms *internal rhyme, repetition, rhythm,* and *rhyme scheme*. Explain that in this lesson students will learn what these terms mean and what role they play in poetry.

Teaching Approach

Use of the Handbook

Read aloud the information on repetition on page 460 of the *Reader's Handbook*. Emphasize examples of repetition as you read the excerpt. Then work with students as they read pages 461–463. Ask student volunteers to read aloud the examples of poetry on these pages, emphasizing rhyme, rhythm, and repetition as they go. Return to the poems and examine their rhyme schemes. Discuss what these poetic devices add to poems.

Extend the Handbook

Have students work in pairs to examine repetition, rhyme, and rhythm in the poems they have used throughout the unit. Partners can also identify the rhyme scheme of each poem. Then encourage students to reflect on what they learned in this unit.

Assessment

Ask students:

■ What is the purpose of repetition? rhyme? rhythm?

■ How did this unit affect your understanding of poetry?

WEEK 25

Reading a Play

For use with *Reader's Handbook* pages 472–488, 503, 510

Daily Lessons	Summary*
Lesson 1 **Reading a Play:** **An Overview**	Have students examine the characteristics of drama. Introduce theater terminology, including acts, scenes, and stage directions.
Lesson 2 **Before Reading** **a Play**	Work with students to apply the Before Reading stages of setting a purpose, previewing, and planning to read a play.
Lesson 3 **While Reading** **a Play**	Review During Reading stages with students. Help them explore the strategy of graphic organizers to keep track of characters, plot, and theme in a play.
Lesson 4 **After Reading** **a Play**	Discuss with students the strategy of visualizing and thinking aloud to use after reading drama. Have students create Storyboards to illustrate a play.

*Use these notes to help you teach a mini-lesson or to teach a briefer, shorter version of the lessons for more proficient students.

Lesson Resources

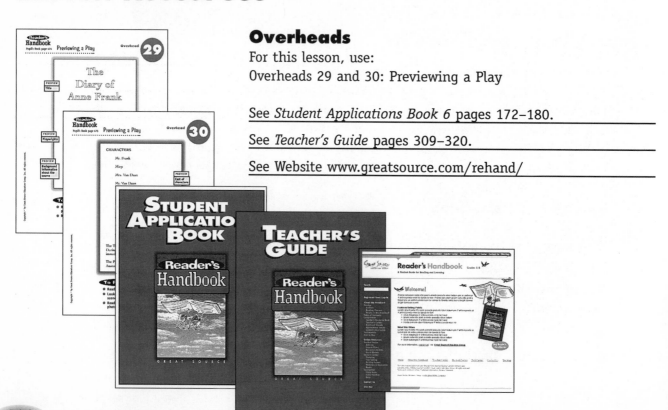

Overheads
For this lesson, use:
Overheads 29 and 30: Previewing a Play

See *Student Applications Book 6* pages 172–180.

See *Teacher's Guide* pages 309–320.

See Website www.greatsource.com/rehand/

Focus on Language

For use with *Reader's Handbook* pages 495–511

Daily Lessons	Summary*
Lesson 1 **Key Lines and Speeches**	Work with students as they examine key lines and speeches in a play. Discuss what these elements add to drama.
Lesson 2 **Stage Directions**	Build an understanding of the importance of stage directions in a play. To demonstrate the purpose of stage directions, have students attempt to read and perform a scene without using them as a guide.
Lesson 3 **Dialogue and Character**	Help students understand the relationship between dialogue and characterization in drama. Have students act out dialogue that reveals important clues about a character's personality.
Lesson 4 **Dialogue, Plot, and Theme**	Discuss with students the relationship between dialogue, plot, and theme. Have students work in small groups to explore this relationship in a play of their choice.

*Use these notes to help you teach a mini-lesson or to teach a briefer, shorter version of the lessons for more proficient students.

Lesson Resources

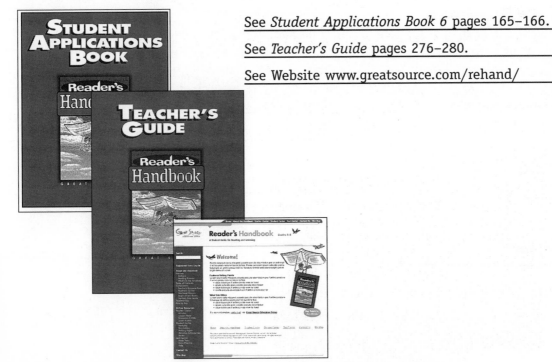

See *Student Applications Book 6* pages 165–166.

See *Teacher's Guide* pages 276–280.

See Website www.greatsource.com/rehand/

WEEK 25
Lesson 1 Reading a Play: An Overview

For use with *Reader's Handbook* pages 472, 484, 503, 510

Goals

In this lesson, students discuss the characteristics of drama and learn theater terminology.

Teaching Focus

Background

As with other forms of fiction, a play can be read using the three stages of the reading process. Plays also contains many of the same elements as short stories and novels—for example, character, setting, plot, and theme. But in other ways, reading a play is very different from reading other forms of fiction. This unit offers students the opportunity to take these more familiar concepts (that is, the reading process, story elements) and apply them to a less familiar genre.

Instruction

Ask students what they know about drama. Have students seen, read, or performed any plays? Discuss the similarities and differences between plays and short stories or novels. Explain that just like these other forms of fiction, a play includes characters, setting, plot, and theme. But unlike these other genres, a play is meant to be performed. Talk about how students think this might change the way a play is written.

Teaching Approach

Use of the Handbook

Read aloud the unit opener on page 472 of the *Reader's Handbook*. Discuss the three goals of the unit. Then work with students as they read about acts and scenes (page 503) and stage directions (page 510). After students have a basic understanding of these concepts, help them understand how plays are organized. Read aloud the first paragraph on page 484. Review the Plot Diagram and the five parts of a plot. Then walk students through the scene breakdown for *The Diary of Anne Frank*.

Extend the Handbook

In their journals, ask students to reflect on their purposes and goals for this unit. They might write about their experiences with or interest in this genre, as well as what they hope to learn about drama from reading this unit.

Assessment

Ask students:

■ How is a play similar to other forms of fiction?

■ In what ways is a play different from other forms of fiction?

■ What is one thing you would like to learn from reading this unit on plays?

WEEK 25
Lesson 2 — Before Reading a Play

For use with *Reader's Handbook* pages 473–476

Goals

In this lesson, students use Before Reading steps to prepare themselves for reading drama.

Teaching Focus

Background

Although the reading process can be applied to a wide variety of texts, different types of writing call for different emphases; thus, students need to adapt the reading process to fit the needs of particular genres. In this unit, students will see how Before Reading, During Reading, and After Reading stages can be adapted for use with a play.

Instruction

Review the Before Reading stage of the reading process. Discuss with students what purposes readers might have for reading drama. Ask students: How will previewing a play differ from other forms of fiction? In what ways will the process be similar?

Teaching Approach

Use of the Handbook

Have a student volunteer read aloud the top of page 473 of the *Reader's Handbook*. Discuss the three questions to ask when setting a purpose. Then have students preview the play and plan for reading independently (pages 473–476). Come together as a class and ask students to share what they learned from the preview.

Extend the Handbook

Gather examples of drama for students to explore, such as *Tales from Shakespeare* by Charles and Mary Lamb. Ask students to choose a play (or an excerpt from a play) to preview. Remind students to refer to the Preview Checklist on page 473 as they work. Have students share what they learned about the drama from previewing with a partner.

For more practice, see pages 172–180 of the *Student Applications Book 6*.

Assessment

Ask students:

■ What questions do readers typically expect a play to answer?

■ How will you use what you learned in this lesson the next time you read plays?

WEEK 25
Lesson 3 — While Reading a Play

For use with *Reader's Handbook* pages 477–483, 485

Goals

In this lesson, students apply the During Reading steps to a drama and explore how graphic organizers can help them keep track of characters, plot, and theme.

Teaching Focus

Background

As discussed in the previous lesson, continually reviewing and applying the reading process to different texts enables students to read various genres more fluently and to use strategies flexibly. This lesson combines the familiar steps of the During Reading stage of the reading process with specific strategies and tools that are useful for reading drama.

Instruction

Review with students how to read with a purpose and connect as they read. Explain that one of the more difficult aspects of reading a play is keeping track of what happens. Discuss the purpose of graphic organizers. Point out that they can be used to help readers summarize and keep track of what's happening (and to whom it is happening) as they read drama.

Teaching Approach

Use of the Handbook

Read aloud or have student volunteers read aloud page 477 of the handbook. Then have students read the excerpt from *The Diary of Anne Frank* on pages 478–480 independently. Discuss the notes and how they connect to the purpose for reading. Then divide the class into three groups. Assign groups one of the following: Magnet Summary (pages 476 and 481), Scene-by-Scene Summary Notes (page 482), and Character Map (page 483). Have each group summarize one tool for the rest of the class. Finish by reading aloud page 485.

Extend the Handbook

In order for students to understand the distinctions among these tools, have them apply them to the play they previewed in the previous lesson. Then have students work in small groups to discuss their thoughts about the organizers. Students might consider the following questions: Which tool seemed to help you the most? Why? What differences did you notice among the tools? How will you decide which to use in the future?

Assessment

Ask students:

■ Choose one tool discussed in this lesson. What is its purpose?

■ How can graphic organizers help you summarize a play?

WEEK 25
Lesson 4 — After Reading a Play

For use with *Reader's Handbook* pages 486–488

Goals

In this lesson, students explore activities, including visualizing and thinking aloud, to use after reading a play.

Teaching Focus

Background

As with other genres, pausing to reflect and rereading will help students develop a deeper understanding and appreciation of dramatic material. In this lesson, students visualize and think aloud to reflect on the meaning of a play.

Instruction

Review the After Reading stage of the reading process with students. (See pages 35–37 of the *Reader's Handbook* for more information.) Ask student volunteers to describe ways they might apply the strategy of visualizing and thinking aloud after reading a play. How do students think this strategy will help them understand a play?

Teaching Approach

Use of the Handbook

Read aloud page 486 of the *Reader's Handbook*, calling students' attention to the Looking Back Checklist. Work with students to understand the strategy of visualizing and thinking aloud (page 487). Discuss how visualizing can enhance students' understanding of a play. Have students create their own Storyboards for Act One of *The Diary of Anne Frank*. Discuss how students' Storyboards compare to the example. Then have students read page 488 independently.

Extend the Handbook

Have students follow the After Reading steps for the play they have been using throughout the unit. Ask them to create Storyboards, such as the one shown on page 487 of the handbook. Encourage students to share their Storyboards with a partner.

Assessment

Ask students:

■ What can you do after reading a play to help you understand it?

■ What is the purpose of visualizing and thinking aloud after reading drama?

■ Compare what you do after reading a play to what you do after reading another form of fiction, such as a poem or a short story. What is the same? What is different?

WEEK 26
Lesson 1 Key Lines and Speeches

For use with *Reader's Handbook* pages 495–496

Goals

In this lesson, students examine key lines and speeches in drama and what these elements add to the play.

Teaching Focus

Background

Examining the language of a play is crucial to understanding its characters, plot, and themes. This unit will offer suggestions and activities to help students explore these elements of drama. This first lesson emphasizes the importance of determining key lines and speeches.

Instruction

Discuss with students why it is important to pay attention to language when reading drama. Explain that since plays do not contain the descriptive details about characters, plot, and theme that stories do, readers must rely on the language of the play to reveal these story elements. Point out that one way to focus on dramatic language is to pay close attention to key lines and speeches.

Teaching Approach

Use of the Handbook

Read aloud the unit opener on page 495 of the *Reader's Handbook*. Discuss the three goals of this section. Then have students work in pairs to read page 496. Encourage pairs to take turns reading the lines from *The Diary of Anne Frank* aloud. Discuss as a class what the language of the two excerpts reveals about the play's meaning.

Extend the Handbook

Have students work in small groups to examine key lines and speeches from one of the plays they have been using throughout this unit. Help students determine what qualifies as a key line by encouraging them to first think about what "big idea" the play explores (i.e., its theme), and then find lines that support this "big idea."

For more practice, see pages 172–180 of the *Student Applications Book 6*.

Assessment

Ask students:

■ Why is it important to examine the language of a play?

■ How can you use key lines and speeches to identify the theme(s) of a play?

WEEK 26
Lesson 2 — Stage Directions

For use with *Reader's Handbook* pages 497 and 510

Goals

In this lesson, students examine the importance of stage directions in a play.

Teaching Focus

Background

Proficient readers understand that stage directions guide a drama and often provide subtle hints about characters' motivations and personalities. Stage directions also play an important role in that they enable readers to visualize the play as they read.

Instruction

Review with students what they learned about stage directions in Week 25, Lesson 1. Ask student volunteers to describe what they think the purpose of stage directions is. Discuss what students do when they come across stage directions in a play. Do they skip over them to get to the action? Explain that stage directions guide the play; paying attention to them helps readers "see" the play in their minds.

Teaching Approach

Use of the Handbook

Ask students to review the information on stage directions on page 510 of the *Reader's Handbook*. Then read aloud the first paragraph on page 497. Have students read the first excerpt to themselves, skipping over the stage directions. Then have them reread the excerpt, this time paying attention to the stage directions. Discuss what the stage directions add to their understanding of the excerpt. Have student volunteers read aloud the rest of page 497. Discuss the importance of the stage directions in the second excerpt.

Extend the Handbook

Stage directions are also important for actors. To illustrate this, have students work in small groups to act out scenes from one of the plays they have been using in this unit. Have actors first perform the scene without using stage directions. Then have them repeat the scene, this time using the stage directions as a guide. Discuss the differences in the two performances.

Assessment

Ask students:

■ What are stage directions?

■ What do stage directions add to a play?

WEEK 26
Lesson 3
Dialogue and Character

For use with *Reader's Handbook* pages 498–499, 505

Goals

In this lesson, students examine the use of dramatic dialogue to reveal character.

Teaching Focus

Background

With the exception of stage directions, drama is made up entirely of dialogue. Although stage directions can tell readers something about characters, playwrights rely predominantly on dialogue to reveal their characters' personalities and motivations. Students will benefit from a close examination of the relationship between dialogue and character.

Instruction

Ask student volunteers to describe what sets drama apart from other forms of fiction. Point out that one of the key distinctions is the use of dialogue. Explain that while stories typically contain some dialogue, plays consist almost entirely of it. Discuss what role dialogue plays in drama. Lead students to see that playwrights rely on dialogue to tell their readers about their characters.

Teaching Approach

Use of the Handbook

Have students read the description of dialogue on page 505 of the *Reader's Handbook*. Then read aloud the top of page 498. Ask student volunteers to take on the roles of Anne and Mr. Van Daan and act out the excerpt. Discuss with the class what the dialogue reveals about the characters. Explore the use of the Double-entry Journal (page 499) to help readers reflect on what dialogue reveals about characters.

Extend the Handbook

Invite students to work in small groups to act out key parts of a play and explore what the dialogue reveals about characters. Have students return to one of the dramas they have used throughout the unit. To help students identify what parts to use, remind them to look for lines that tell them something about a character's personality or motivations.

For more practice, see pages 183–184 of the *Student Applications Book 6*.

Assessment

Ask students:

■ Why do playwrights rely on dialogue to reveal characters' personalities?

■ How can a Double-entry Journal help you reflect on a play's dialogue?

WEEK 26
Lesson 4 Dialogue, Plot, and Theme

For use with *Reader's Handbook* pages 499–500, 507–508, 511

Goals

In this lesson, students explore the relationship between dialogue, plot, and theme in drama.

Teaching Focus

Background

Drama contains the same story elements as other forms of fiction. And just as in these other forms, readers need to follow the action of the plot and identify themes in order to find meaning. Examining what dialogue can reveal about a play's plot and themes will enable students to get more out of reading a play.

Instruction

Review with students what they know about plot and theme from their work on short stories and novels. Explain that plays contain these story elements as well. Point out that playwrights rely on dialogue to guide the play's action and to reveal its themes.

Teaching Approach

Use of the Handbook

Have students work in pairs to read the descriptions of plot and theme in a play on pages 507–508 and 511 of the *Reader's Handbook*. Come together as a class and discuss what themes are revealed in the excerpt on page 511. Then read aloud the information on dialogue and plot on page 499. Ask a student volunteer to read the top paragraph on page 500. Work with students to identify the theme(s) revealed in the short excerpt on this page.

Extend the Handbook

Have students work in small groups to discuss the plot and themes of some of the dramas they have worked with throughout this unit. Ask groups to find examples of dialogue that reveal information about the plot and theme. Then have groups discuss what they discovered about plays from this unit.

For practice, see pages 181–184 of the *Student Applications Book 6*.

Assessment

Ask students:

■ What is the relationship between dialogue, plot, and theme in a play?

■ What is the most important thing you learned about plays from this unit?

WEEK 27

Reading a Website

For use with *Reader's Handbook* pages 514–526

Daily Lessons	Summary*
Lesson 1 **Before Reading a Website**	Discuss with students the importance of setting a purpose, previewing, and planning before reading a website. Have students choose a topic to research and preview a website related to their topic.
Lesson 2 **Reading a Website Critically**	Work with students as they explore methods of reading websites critically, including creating a Website Profiler and taking notes.
Lesson 3 **How Websites Are Organized**	Build an understanding of the organization of websites to help students get the most out of their reading.
Lesson 4 **Evaluating Internet Sources**	Explore with students After Reading activities for evaluating Internet sources, including rereading and skimming. Students visit a site and create a written evaluation of it.

*Use these notes to help you teach a mini-lesson or to teach a briefer, shorter version of the lessons for more proficient students.

Lesson Resources

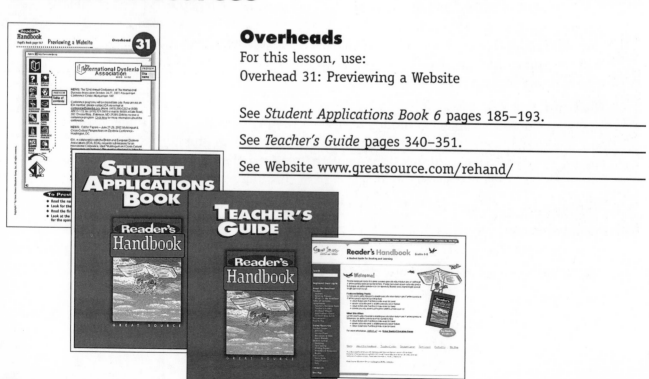

Overheads
For this lesson, use:
Overhead 31: Previewing a Website

See *Student Applications Book 6* pages 185–193.

See *Teacher's Guide* pages 340–351.

See Website www.greatsource.com/rehand/

WEEK 28

Elements of the Internet

For use with *Reader's Handbook* pages 527–535

Daily Lessons	Summary*
Lesson 1 **Browsers, Bookmarks, and Links**	Introduce three Internet elements: browsers, bookmarks, and links.
Lesson 2 **Sending Email**	Work with students to define the characteristics of email and its uses. Remind students to never give personal information on the Internet.
Lesson 3 **Using Search Engines**	Build an understanding of search engines, and explore strategies for searching the Internet more effectively.
Lesson 4 **The World Wide Web**	Help students understand what the World Wide Web is. Examine its features, including the use of URLs and hypertext.

*Use these notes to help you teach a mini-lesson or to teach a briefer, shorter version of the lessons for more proficient students.

Lesson Resources

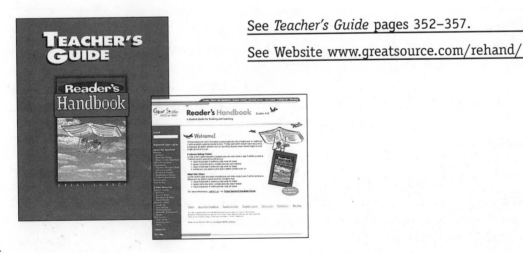

See *Teacher's Guide* pages 352–357.

See Website www.greatsource.com/rehand/

WEEK 27
Lesson 1

Before Reading a Website

For use with *Reader's Handbook* pages 514–518

Goals

In this lesson, students discuss the importance of setting a purpose, previewing, and planning before reading a website.

Teaching Focus

Background

The Internet offers us almost unlimited information. All too often, however, users get lost in cyberspace, moving from link to link without having a clear purpose in mind. In order to get the most out of their time spent on the Internet, students need to be able to set a purpose, preview, and plan their reading.

Instruction

Discuss with students what they know about websites. You might create a Concept Map for *website* to list students' responses. (See page 670 for an example of a Concept Map.) Explain that in this unit students will learn strategies that will help them use websites more effectively. Talk about reasons why people use websites. Point out that using the Internet to gather information requires different strategies than surfing the Web for fun does; this unit emphasizes strategies for gathering information.

Teaching Approach

Use of the Handbook

Read aloud the unit opener on page 514 of the *Reader's Handbook*. Review the unit's goals with students. Then have students work in small groups to read about setting a purpose on pages 515–516. Help students understand the importance of setting a purpose and sticking to that purpose throughout their work on the website. Then have groups read the information under the preview and plan steps on pages 516–518.

Extend the Handbook

Ask students to brainstorm a list of topics that they would like to learn more about. Invite them to choose one topic to explore during this unit, and have them brainstorm a list of questions they have about the topic. Help them find an appropriate website for their topic, and then have them preview the site using the Preview Checklist on page 516.

Assessment

Ask students:

■ Why is it important to set a purpose before reading a website?

■ What do you hope to learn about websites and the Internet from this unit?

WEEK 27
Lesson 2 Reading a Website Critically

For use with *Reader's Handbook* pages 518–522

Goals

In this lesson, students explore the strategy of reading websites critically, including creating a Website Profiler and taking notes.

Teaching Focus

Background

There is no governing body to determine the accuracy of a website; it is the user's responsibility to do so. In order to achieve this, students need step-by-step instructions on reading websites critically. This can be difficult for students at first, but it is the single, most important strategy for using the Internet effectively.

Instruction

Ask students who they think creates websites. Point out that anyone can create a website; moreover, website creators can say anything they want, even if it is not true. Discuss with students what this means for Internet users. Lead them to see that users must read websites critically to evaluate the information presented.

Teaching Approach

Use of the Handbook

Read aloud the information on reading critically on page 518 of the *Reader's Handbook*. Then work with students as they explore the tools for reading critically on page 519. Discuss the Website Profiler and how it can help students determine the accuracy of a site. Then have students work in pairs to read pages 520–522. Come together as a class and discuss how keeping their purposes in mind and taking notes can help students read critically.

Extend the Handbook

Have students create a Website Profiler for the website they previewed in the previous lesson. Then have students read the information on the website, keeping their purpose in mind. Encourage students to take notes. Remind them to use their own words and to use quotation marks around exact quotes.

For more practice, see pages 185–193 of the *Student Applications Book 6*.

Assessment

Ask students:

■ Why is it important to read websites critically?

■ What reading tools can you use as you to read websites critically?

WEEK 27
Lesson 3 — How Websites Are Organized

For use with *Reader's Handbook* page 522

Goals

In this lesson, students examine how understanding the organization of websites can help them get the most out of their reading.

Teaching Focus

Background

The organization of websites is markedly different from the organization of books. Students are most likely more familiar with the page-by-page organization of books; websites, with their numerous links, are much more complicated. Understanding how websites are organized will provide a framework to help students navigate sites.

Instruction

Work with students to compare the characteristics of websites and books. Explain that both books and websites are made up of pages. The key difference is how these pages are organized. Ask a student volunteer to create a sketch to represent how a book is organized. Then invite another volunteer to create a sketch to represent how a website might be organized. Discuss which sketch was easier to create. Point out that websites are organized in a more complex way than books; identifying the organization will help students stay on track as they read.

Teaching Approach

Use of the Handbook

Read aloud or have a student volunteer read aloud the information under "How Websites Are Organized" on page 522 of the *Reader's Handbook*. Have students compare the sketches created above with the sketches in the handbook. Discuss their similarities and differences.

Extend the Handbook

Have students examine the organization of the website they have been using throughout the unit. Ask them to create a sketch to illustrate its organization. Encourage students to share their sketches with a partner. Are the two websites organized similarly? What do the sketches tell them about the websites?

Assessment

Ask students:

■ How is the organization of websites different from that of books?

■ How does knowing the organization of a website help you read it?

■ Which organization makes for easier reading? Why?

WEEK 27
Lesson 4   Evaluating Internet Sources

For use with *Reader's Handbook* page 525

Goals

In this lesson, students discuss the After Reading steps, including rereading and the strategy of skimming, that can be used to evaluate Internet sources.

Teaching Focus

Background

Reading critically and evaluating are closely linked. Lesson 2 showed students how to how use the strategy of reading critically with websites; this lesson walks students through the steps involved in rereading and using the rereading strategy of skimming a website in order to evaluate its reliability.

Instruction

Review with students the importance of reading websites critically. Explain that after visiting a website, students should reread and evaluate its information to be sure it is reliable and fair. What do students think are the benefits of rereading a website?

Teaching Approach

Use of the Handbook

Read aloud the top of page 525 of the *Reader's Handbook*. Then ask student volunteers to read aloud each step in the checklist. Pause in between steps to talk about what each step will tell students about the accuracy of the site's information. After reading, have students compare the checklist with the Website Profiler on page 519. How are these tools similar? How are they different?

Extend the Handbook

Have students use the checklist on page 525 of the handbook to evaluate the information presented on the website they have been using throughout the unit. Ask them to take notes about what they discover as they go. Encourage them to use their notes to write an evaluation about the accuracy of the site.

For more practice, see pages 185–193 of the *Student Applications Book 6*.

Assessment

Ask students:

■ What questions can you ask after visiting a website to help you evaluate it?

■ Why is it important to evaluate the information on a website?

Browsers, Bookmarks, and Links

For use with *Reader's Handbook* pages 528, 529, 532

Goals

In this lesson, students learn about three Internet elements: browsers, bookmarks, and links.

Teaching Focus

Background

In order to get the most out of the Internet, students need a general understanding of its elements. This unit will introduce students to some of these elements, beginning with an explanation of browsers, bookmarks, and links. Some students will be familiar with these elements while this may be other students' first exposure to them. Modify the lessons as necessary to suit students' needs.

Instruction

Show students a paper bookmark. Ask student volunteers to describe it. Discuss the purpose of bookmarks. Point out that people use bookmarks when they surf the Internet as well. Then write the word *browser* on the board. Discuss what it means to browse. Repeat this procedure with the term *link*. Explain that in this lesson students will learn more about bookmarks, browsers, and links and what they mean.

Teaching Approach

Use of the Handbook

Divide the class into three groups. Have one group read the information on bookmarks (page 528), one group read about browsers (page 529), and the last group read about links (page 532). Ask groups to share what they learned about the element with the rest of the class. Make sure students understand why each element is helpful to Internet users.

Extend the Handbook

Have students explore the use of bookmarks and links on their own. Ask them to return to the website they have been working with throughout this unit. First, help them create a bookmark for their website. Then have them explore the links on the site. Remind students that jumping from link to link can be confusing. Discuss tools they can use to help them keep track of their movement.

Assessment

Ask students:

■ What is a browser? a bookmark? a link?

■ What is the purpose of each?

180

WEEK 28
Lesson 2 Sending Email

For use with *Reader's Handbook* pages 530–531

Goals

In this lesson, students explore the characteristics of email and its uses.

Teaching Focus

Background

Email is fast becoming one of our most common forms of communication. Students will benefit from an examination of the organization and characteristics of email, as well as a discussion of the advantages and disadvantages of chat rooms and instant messaging.

Instruction

Assess students' familiarity with email by asking how many have used it recently. Explain that in some ways, sending an email is similar to writing a letter, but that email has its own unique features as well as its own etiquette. Then ask students what they know about chat rooms. Explain that in this lesson students will learn more about emails and chat rooms and other ways of "instant messaging."

Teaching Approach

Use of the Handbook

Walk students through the sample email on page 530 of the *Reader's Handbook*. Point out its format, including the header, body, and address. Review the standard components of an email address. Ask student volunteers to provide examples of email addresses with which they are familiar, pointing out the commonality of their basic parts. Then have a student volunteer read aloud the information on chat rooms on page 531. Discuss the advantages and disadvantages of chat rooms. Lead students to see that one of the biggest disadvantages is that there is no way of knowing if people are telling the truth in their emails and instant messages. Discuss why students should not give out any personal information on the Internet.

Extend the Handbook

To practice using standard email formatting, have students send email messages to one another. Remind students to fill out the header completely, including the subject and the receivers' full address. You might want to spend some time discussing email etiquette, including not using all caps and not forwarding others' email without their consent.

Assessment

Ask students:

■ What are the two main parts of an email address?

■ What should you watch out for when visiting a chat room?

WEEK 28
Lesson 3 — Using Search Engines

For use with *Reader's Handbook* page 533

Goals

In this lesson, students learn about search engines and explore techniques for searching the Internet more effectively.

Teaching Focus

Background

Search engines are wonderful tools for finding information on the Internet. But unless users understand how to search effectively, searches can end up with over one million matches. An exploration of the purposes of search engines as well as a discussion of techniques for using them will enable students to use them more effectively.

Instruction

Ask students to guess how many websites the Internet contains. Point out that there are millions of websites and more are added every day. Discuss how students find information on a topic when they use the Internet. Explain that Internet users often rely on search engines to help them locate information related to a specific topic.

Teaching Approach

Use of the Handbook

Have students skim page 533 of the *Reader's Handbook*. Then walk them through the sample search engine home page. Point out the standard features of search engines, including a web address, space to type in key words, and links to other sites. Have student volunteers read aloud the description and definition of search engines.

Extend the Handbook

Spend some time discussing methods for searching the Internet effectively. Explain that the more specific students are when typing in their key words, the more specific their results will be. To illustrate this, have students use a search engine, such as Google (www.google.com) to search for websites on the topic they have been working on throughout this unit. First, have them type in the general topic and note the number of matches. Then help them refine their search by brainstorming key words that would most closely match their search. Compare the number and quality of matches generated by the general and the refined search.

Assessment

Ask students:

■ What is the purpose of search engines?

■ How can you use search engines effectively?

WEEK 28
Lesson 4 — The World Wide Web

For use with *Reader's Handbook* pages 534–535

Goals

In this lesson, students examine the World Wide Web and its features.

Teaching Focus

Background

The introduction of the World Wide Web in 1990 has resulted in an explosion of information on the Internet. Today, the Web is by far the most popular part of the Internet. Its use of hypertext enables users to get to where they want to go with ease; the more students understand the Web, the more they will be able to use it to its fullest potential.

Instruction

Discuss with students their understanding of the World Wide Web. What do students think it is? How does it work? Explain that the World Wide Web is a huge system of computers from around the world that share files. Point out that in this section of the handbook, students will learn more about the World Wide Web and some of its characteristics, including the use of hypertext and URLs.

Teaching Approach

Use of the Handbook

Work with students to analyze the sample home page on page 534 of the *Reader's Handbook*. Point out its key features, such as the URL and hypertext. Then read aloud the description of the World Wide Web on page 535. Discuss the specialized vocabulary, including *home page*, *web page*, and *links*. Explain that paying attention to a website's URL can tell users something about the site's purpose: for example, .com refers to commercial sites, .edu refers to educational sites, and .org is used for non-profit organizations.

Extend the Handbook

Have students explore the World Wide Web independently. If your school district has a website, ask students to begin there. Encourage them to look for examples of hypertext and to investigate links. Have students use what they have learned throughout the unit as they explore.

Assessment

Ask students:

■ What is the World Wide Web?

■ What is the most important thing you learned from this unit? Explain your answer.

Reading a Graphic

For use with *Reader's Handbook* pages 537–547

Daily Lessons	Summary*
Lesson 1 **Before Reading a Graphic**	Discuss with students the importance of setting a purpose, previewing, and planning before reading a graphic. Students choose a graphic to explore throughout the unit.
Lesson 2 **Reading Graphics: Paraphrasing for Understanding**	Build an understanding of the importance of paraphrasing when reading graphics. Have students paraphrase and create a Double-entry Journal for graphic.
Lesson 3 **How Graphics Are Organized**	Work with students as they explore the organization of graphics. Discuss how understanding a graphic's organization can help students use the graphic more effectively.
Lesson 4 **Evaluating Graphics: Reading Critically and Drawing Conclusions**	Discuss with students the roles reading critically and drawing conclusions play in evaluating graphic sources.

*Use these notes to help you teach a mini-lesson or to teach a briefer, shorter version of the lessons for more proficient students.

Lesson Resources

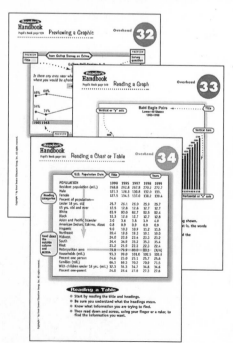

Overheads

For this lesson, use:

Overhead 32: Previewing a Graphic

Overhead 33: Reading a Graph

Overhead 34: Reading a Chart or Table

See *Student Applications Book 6* pages 194–199.

See *Teacher's Guide* pages 359–369.

See Website www.greatsource.com/rehand/

Elements of Graphics For use with *Reader's Handbook* pages 548–561

Daily Lessons	Summary*
Lesson 1 **Reading Cartoons**	Discuss the purpose of cartoons. Help students apply the reading process to cartoons.
Lesson 2 **Reading Diagrams**	Work with students to explore how to read a diagram.
Lesson 3 **Reading Maps**	Build an understanding of the five main types of maps. Work with students to explore techniques for reading maps successfully.
Lesson 4 **Reading Tables**	Discuss with students the purposes and characteristics of tables. Walk them through techniques for reading tables.

*Use these notes to help you teach a mini-lesson or to teach a briefer, shorter version of the lessons for more proficient students.

Lesson Resources

See *Teacher's Guide* pages 370–377.

See Website www.greatsource.com/rehand/

WEEK 29
Lesson 1 — Before Reading a Graphic

For use with *Reader's Handbook* pages 538–540

Goals

In this lesson, students examine ways of applying Before Reading steps to graphics.

Teaching Focus

Background

The ability to interpret and evaluate information in graphics is crucial for fully understanding nonfiction texts. All too often, students skip over the graphics, unaware that they provide valuable information. In addition, students may be unfamiliar with tips for reading graphics. The lessons in this unit will provide them with specific techniques for reading graphics effectively.

Instruction

Activate students' prior knowledge of graphics by initiating a discussion about graphics in general. Work with students to brainstorm types of graphics, such as bar graphs, pie charts, and timelines. Discuss the purpose of these graphics. Then talk about what students do when they come across a graphic in their reading. Explain that the reading process for reading graphics is similar to the process used for reading text; applying the reading process to graphics will help students make sense of them.

Teaching Approach

Use of the Handbook

Read the unit opener on page 538 of the *Reader's Handbook*. Review the unit's goals with students. Ask a student volunteer to read aloud the information under Set a Purpose. Discuss the two questions to keep in mind when reading a graphic. Model the step of previewing by thinking aloud as you explore the graphic on page 539. Then walk students through the five steps for reading a graphic on page 540.

Extend the Handbook

Gather a variety of graphics for students to explore throughout the unit. (The local newspaper should provide you with quite a few, or students can use graphics from their social studies or science textbooks.) Ask students to work in pairs to set a purpose, preview, and plan for reading the graphic.

Assessment

Ask students:

■ Why do you set a purpose, preview, and plan before reading a graphic?

■ What do you hope to learn about reading graphics from this unit?

WEEK 29
Lesson 2

Reading Graphics: Paraphrasing for Understanding

For use with *Reader's Handbook* pages 539–541; 544

Goals

In this lesson, students examine the strategy of paraphrasing when reading graphics.

Teaching Focus

Background

Paraphrasing is a useful strategy for reading graphics because it requires students to examine the information in the graphic and then process and reflect on it. Paraphrasing will also help students remember the information in graphics. Students will benefit from a discussion of the importance of paraphrasing, as well as a general overview of techniques for applying During Reading strategies to graphics.

Instruction

Discuss what students know about paraphrasing. Explain that to paraphrase something means to put it into one's own words. Have students predict why a unit on reading graphics would include a section on paraphrasing. What role do students think paraphrasing plays when reading graphics?

Teaching Approach

Use of the Handbook

Read aloud the information on paraphrasing on page 540 of the *Reader's Handbook*. Then encourage students working in pairs to try to paraphrase the graphic on page 539. Have students continue to work in pairs and read page 541. Make sure students take the time to compare their paraphrases to the example on this page. Then ask pairs to read page 544. Have them create Paraphrase Charts, using the example as a guide.

Extend the Handbook

Have students paraphrase the information in the graphic they selected in the previous lesson. Encourage them to create Paraphrase Charts for the information as well.

For more practice, see pages 194–199 of the *Student Applications Book 6*.

Assessment

Ask students:

■ How do you paraphrase information?

■ How does paraphrasing help you understand the information in a graphic?

WEEK 29
Lesson 3 — How Graphics Are Organized

For use with *Reader's Handbook* pages 542–543

Goals

In this lesson, students enhance their understanding of information presented graphically by examining the organization of graphics.

Teaching Focus

Background

Although graphics can be organized in a number of ways, most share some common characteristics, such as titles, axes, and legends. Understanding these characteristics and what their functions are will enable students to interpret and evaluate the information in graphics more effectively.

Instruction

Ask student volunteers to identify key parts of the graphics they have been using throughout the unit. Lead them to see that while graphics can be organized in a variety of ways, they do have some characteristics in common. Discuss with students why it is important to understand how a graphic is organized.

Teaching Approach

Use of the Handbook

Build an understanding of how graphics can be organized by reading aloud the information on page 542 of the *Reader's Handbook*. Point out the key features of the sample graphic. Explain the purpose of each feature. Then have students read page 543 independently. Encourage students to paraphrase the information on "Finding the Axes" and "Finding the Legend."

Extend the Handbook

Ask students to examine the organization of the graphic they have been using throughout the unit. Have them label its key features using sticky notes or highlighting. Come together as a class and discuss how concentrating on the way the graphic is organized affected students' understanding of it.

For more practice, see pages 194–199 in the *Student Applications Book 6*.

Assessment

Ask students:

■ What is the purpose of a legend?

■ How does knowing the organization of a graphic help you to read it?

WEEK 29
Lesson 4

Evaluating Graphics: Reading Critically and Drawing Conclusions

For use with *Reader's Handbook* pages 545–547

Goals

In this lesson, students examine the roles reading critically and drawing conclusions play in evaluating graphic sources.

Teaching Focus

Background

Once students understand the information in a graphic, they need to take their learning one step further. In order to use the information effectively, readers must draw conclusions about both what the information means and its reliability. A critical reading of graphics will enable readers to draw accurate conclusions.

Instruction

Review with students the two questions they asked before reading (see page 538). Explain that to answer them completely, readers need to apply the rereading strategy of reading critically. Activate prior knowledge by reviewing what students know about this strategy.

Teaching Approach

Use of the Handbook

Read aloud the information under "Reading Critically" on page 545 of the *Reader's Handbook*. Then walk students through the steps involved when drawing conclusions about graphic sources. Discuss the importance of identifying what information is left out. How can this help students determine if the graphic is biased or not?

Extend the Handbook

Have students apply the four steps for drawing conclusions to the graphic they have been working with throughout this unit. Ask them to use their conclusions to answer the two Setting a Purpose questions.

For more practice, see pages 194–199 of the *Student Applications Book 6*.

Assessment

Ask students:

■ What question can you ask to draw conclusions about and evaluate the information in a graphic?

■ Why is it important to pay attention to missing information when evaluating a graphic?

WEEK 30
Lesson 1 — Reading Cartoons

For use with *Reader's Handbook* pages 550–551

Goals

In this lesson, students examine cartoons and their characteristics.

Teaching Focus

Background

Students are probably aware that cartoons are a vehicle for humor, but do they know that cartoons can also be a valuable tool for expressing an opinion? In order to understand a cartoon's message, however, readers need to know how to read it. In this lesson, students will learn how to use a step-by-step approach to understanding and evaluating cartoons.

Instruction

Show a cartoon to students. Ask student volunteers to explain what the purpose of cartoons is. Lead students to see that unlike comic strips, cartoons, particularly editorial cartoons, are meant to express opinions as well as to entertain. Talk about reasons why cartoonists use cartoons to make their point instead of other methods of persuasion. What do students think are the advantages of using cartoons?

Teaching Approach

Use of the Handbook

Have students examine the cartoon on page 550. What do students think it means? Explain that there are techniques for reading cartoons that make them easier to understand. Walk students through the steps for reading cartoons (pages 550–551). Discuss *irony* and its use in cartoons. Then have students use the steps to revisit the cartoon on page 550. Does following the steps deepen their understanding? Discuss.

Extend the Handbook

Gather examples of editorial and political cartoons. (Syd Hoff's *Editorial and Political Cartooning* contains 700 examples from master cartoonists.) Have students work in pairs to analyze two or three cartoons using the steps listed on pages 550–551. Ask them to choose one cartoon to present to the class. Have partners state what is happening in the cartoon in their own words. Encourage them to discuss the cartoon's message. What is the cartoon saying about its subject?

Assessment

Ask students:

■ What is the purpose of cartoons?

■ What techniques can you use for reading cartoons effectively?

■ How do these techniques affect your understanding of cartoons?

WEEK 30
Lesson 2   Reading Diagrams

For use with *Reader's Handbook* pages 552–553

Goals

In this lesson, students examine diagrams and strategies for reading them.

Teaching Focus

Background

Diagrams are one of the more straightforward graphics available to readers. Typically, diagrams are used in conjunction with text, either to illustrate how something works or to label its parts. Understanding a diagram can help students deepen their understanding of the reading material in general. While diagrams tend to be easier to comprehend than other more sophisticated graphics, students will still benefit from reviewing techniques for reading them successfully.

Instruction

Remind students of their brainstorming session from Week 29, Lesson 1. Review their list of graphics. Explain that different graphics have different purposes. Point out that some graphics are used to compare information while others are used to show quantities. Explain that in this lesson students will learn more about diagrams, a common graphic used to label the parts of something or to show how something works.

Teaching Approach

Use of the Handbook

Read aloud the first paragraph on page 552 of the *Reader's Handbook*. Have students look over the diagram. Then discuss what they think its purpose is. Lead them to see that the diagram helps readers see the layers and structures of human skin. Walk students through the steps for reading a diagram on pages 552–553. Then have them apply these steps to the diagrams shown on these pages. Talk about how the suggestions helped them make sense of the diagrams.

Extend the Handbook

Have students look through social studies or science textbooks for examples of diagrams. Ask them to choose one to explore, using the strategies from the handbook. Remind students to read the text that accompanies the diagram as well in order to better understand what is being described.

Assessment

Ask students:

■ What is the purpose of a diagram?

■ What techniques can you use to better understand a diagram?

WEEK 30
Lesson 3 Reading a Map

For use with *Reader's Handbook* pages 555–556

Goals

In this lesson, students explore the characteristics of the five main types of maps and discuss the process of reading them.

Teaching Focus

Background

In order to read maps effectively, proficient readers rely on specific techniques, including identifying the map's type and examining its legend and scale. A discussion of the purpose of maps and their characteristics will enable students to get the most out of this kind of graphic.

Instruction

Work with students to create a Concept Map (see page 670 of the *Reader's Handbook* for more information on Concept Maps). Include the different kinds of maps with which students are familiar, as well as common map features. Discuss the purposes of maps. Explain that there are specific techniques for reading maps that will help students use them successfully.

Teaching Approach

Use of the Handbook

Have students explore the map on page 555 of the *Reader's Handbook*. What information does this map provide? What is its purpose? Then read aloud the top of page 556. Walk students through the five main types of maps, and discuss the purpose of each. Then introduce the techniques for reading maps on the bottom of page 556. Have students apply these techniques to the map on page 555. Discuss how using these techniques helped them better understand what the map is all about.

Extend the Handbook

Have students create their own maps. They might concentrate on their immediate neighborhood or the area around the school. Encourage students to first identify the type of map they will create and its purpose. Remind students to include a title, legend, and scale (approximate). Have students share their maps with a partner. Ask partners to use the map-reading techniques to make sense of each other's maps.

Assessment

Ask students:

■ What are the five main types of maps?

■ What techniques can you use to read maps effectively?

192

WEEK 30
Lesson 4 ▸ Reading Tables

For use with *Reader's Handbook* pages 559–560

Goals

In this lesson, students examine tables and their characteristics.

Teaching Focus

Background

Tables are one of the most common forms of graphics. They can also be one of the most difficult to interpret because they often include numerous statistics that need to be both understood and compared for true comprehension. An examination of the characteristics of tables and strategies for reading them will enable students to deepen their understanding of the information presented.

Instruction

Show students examples of tables, such as those on baseball cards or stock market updates. Talk about the purposes of each sample table. Then discuss what students know about tables. Point out that tables are made up of columns and rows of information. Explain that just as with cartoons, diagrams, and maps, there are steps to follow when reading tables that will help students use them successfully.

Teaching Approach

Use of the Handbook

Have a student volunteer read aloud the top of page 559 of the *Reader's Handbook*. Then think aloud as you examine the sample table. Point out the title, column and row headings, and what information the table contains. Continue thinking aloud as you draw conclusions from the table. Then walk students through the suggestions for reading tables on pages 559–560. Have students apply the techniques to the table on page 560.

Extend the Handbook

Have students look through content area textbooks for examples of other tables. Ask them to choose one to explore in detail. Remind students to use the techniques discussed in this lesson to read the table. Have students summarize the table by identifying what data is presented and what conclusions they can draw from it.

Assessment

Ask students:

■ What techniques can you use to understand the information in tables?

■ What is the most important thing you learned about graphics from this unit? Explain your answer.

Reading a Test and Test Questions

For use with *Reader's Handbook* pages 563–579

Daily Lessons	Summary*
Lesson 1 **Before Reading a Test**	Walk students through Before Reading activities to do before taking a test. Have students create a test-taking guide.
Lesson 2 **Reading a Test: Analyzing Questions**	Build an understanding of the importance of analyzing test questions. Have students continue working on their test-taking guide.
Lesson 3 **Test-Taking Strategy: Skimming**	Discuss with students the role skimming plays when taking a test. Compare skimming for specific information to skimming during a preview.
Lesson 4 **After Reading a Test: Visualizing and Thinking Aloud**	Work with students to examine how visualizing and thinking aloud can help them work through difficult test questions. Have students work in pairs to practice this strategy.

*Use these notes to help you teach a mini-lesson or to teach a briefer, shorter version of the lessons for more proficient students.

Lesson Resources

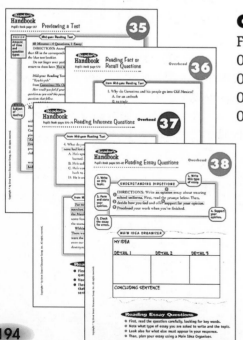

Overheads

For this lesson, use:
Overhead 35: Previewing a Test
Overhead 36: Reading Fact or Recall Questions
Overhead 37: Reading Inference Questions
Overhead 38: Reading Essay Questions

See *Student Applications Book 6* pages 200–207.

See *Teacher's Guide* pages 379–388.

See Website www.greatsource.com/rehand/

WEEK 32

Reading a Test and Test Questions

For use with *Reader's Handbook* pages 563–579

Daily Lessons	Summary*
Lesson 5 **Focus on Vocabulary Tests**	Help students identify techniques to use when preparing for and taking vocabulary tests. Have students create flash cards or vocabulary notebooks for a content area of their choice.
Lesson 6 **Focus on Social Studies Tests**	Work with students to explore techniques for taking social studies tests successfully. Have students create a list of tips to keep in their social studies folders.
Lesson 7 **Focus on Math Tests**	Discuss the techniques students can use to prepare for and take math tests. Review general test-taking strategies, such as crossing out obvious wrong answers.
Lesson 8 **Focus on Science Tests**	Build an understanding of the techniques students can rely on when taking science tests. Review techniques for understanding graphics.

*Use these notes to help you teach a mini-lesson or to teach a briefer, shorter version of the lessons for more proficient students.

Lesson Resources

Overheads
For this lesson, use:
Overhead 35: Previewing a Test
Overhead 36: Reading Fact or Recall Questions
Overhead 37: Reading Inference Questions
Overhead 38: Reading Essay Questions

See *Student Applications Book 6* pages 210–217.

See *Teacher's Guide* pages 379–388.

See Website www.greatsource.com/rehand/

WEEK 31
Lesson 1 Before Reading a Test

For use with *Reader's Handbook* pages 564–570

Goals

In this lesson, students learn how to use Before Reading activities to prepare for a test.

Teaching Focus

Background

Successful test-takers understand that there are techniques that can help them read and perform well on tests. Utilizing the steps in the reading process is one such strategy. Since by now students are quite familiar with the process, they should have little difficulty transferring it to tests. They may have difficulty, however, understanding exactly how the reading process can help. Emphasizing the benefits of using Before Reading, During Reading, and After Reading activities when taking tests will motivate students to rely on the reading process as they work.

Instruction

Discuss test-taking with students. How do students feel about taking tests? What do they do to prepare for tests? Explain that there are specific techniques students can use to help them do well on all kinds of tests. Point out that using the reading process is one such technique. Ask students how they might use the reading process when taking tests. Explain that in this lesson students will learn ways to apply the Before Reading activities to tests.

Teaching Approach

Use of the Handbook

Have students read page 565 of the *Reader's Handbook* independently. Then walk students through the Preview Checklist on page 566. Ask students to preview the test on pages 567–570 using the checklist as a guide. Come together as a class and discuss what students learned from previewing the test.

Extend the Handbook

Have students create a test-taking guide to review before taking tests. Ask them to begin by listing techniques to use before reading a test. Encourage them to be as specific as possible with their tips. (For example, tips such as "Determine the amount of time I have" and "Decide whether to make guesses or not" are more helpful than "Preview the test.")

For more practice, see pages 200–207 of the *Student Applications Book 6.*

Assessment

Ask students:

■ What should you do before reading a test?

■ What do you hope to learn about taking tests from this unit?

WEEK 31
Lesson 2 Reading a Test: Analyzing Questions

For use with *Reader's Handbook* pages 572–576

Goals

In this lesson, students learn techniques for analyzing test questions.

Teaching Focus

Background

In order to perform well on tests, students need to understand that different types of questions require different techniques. An examination of two main types of test questions—fact or recall and inference or conclusion—will enable students to apply the appropriate techniques to each type.

Instruction

Discuss what students know about taking tests successfully. Do they mark up the text as they read? Circle key words? Cross off obvious wrong answers? Explain that these are all smart test-taking techniques. Point out that another test-taking technique is to analyze the questions to determine how to answer them correctly. Then explain that there are two main types of test questions—fact or recall and inference or conclusion. Most tests include a variety of each.

Teaching Approach

Use of the Handbook

Have student volunteers read aloud the information under "Read with a Purpose" on page 572 of the *Reader's Handbook*. Ask students to revisit the sample test on pages 567–570 and apply the techniques discussed in this section to it. Come together as a class and discuss how these techniques affected students' understanding of the material. Then walk students through the suggestions for analyzing the two types of test questions. Compare the process of answering fact or recall questions with that of reading inference or conclusion questions. Then have students read the rest of the section independently.

Extend the Handbook

Have students add to their test-taking guide by listing techniques discussed in this section. Remind students to include the different strategies for reading the two types of test questions.

For more practice, see pages 200–207 of the *Student Applications Book 6*.

Assessment

Ask students:

■ What are the two main types of test questions?

■ How does determining a question's type help you answer the question correctly?

WEEK 31
Lesson 3 Test-Taking Strategy: Skimming

For use with *Reader's Handbook* pages 571

Goals

In this lesson, students discover how the reading strategy of skimming can help them identify important information when they take tests.

Teaching Focus

Background

Successful test-takers understand that skimming is a useful tool for making the most of the test-taking experience. Since effective skimming enables students to find information quickly, this reading strategy is particularly critical for timed tests.

Instruction

Review with students what they know about skimming. Discuss how students use the strategy when they preview a text. Explain that skimming is an important strategy for taking tests as well. Discuss with students the differences between skimming to preview a text and skimming as a test-taking strategy.

For more information on skimming, see pages 656–657 of the *Reader's Handbook*.

Teaching Approach

Use of the Handbook

Have a student volunteer read aloud the information on skimming on page 571 of the *Reader's Handbook*. Model the strategy by thinking aloud as you skim the first page of the sample test (page 567). Then have students work in pairs to take turns skimming the rest of the example (pages 568–570). Come together as a class and discuss what students learned from skimming the test.

Extend the Handbook

For additional practice skimming tests for information, have students work through pages 200–207 of the *Student Applications Book 6*.

Assessment

Ask students:

■ What is the purpose of skimming to find information in a test?

■ What is the difference between skimming as part of the previewing process and skimming for specific information? Explain the differences between the two.

WEEK 31
Lesson 4
After Reading a Test: Visualizing and Thinking Aloud

For use with *Reader's Handbook* pages 576–579

Goals

In this lesson, students examine the role Visualizing and Thinking Aloud plays in answering test questions successfully.

Teaching Focus

Background
Typically, even the most successful test-takers will be stumped by a few questions. In this lesson, students will learn how to review their work at the end of a test and tackle any remaining questions with a new strategy.

Instruction
Discuss with students what they do once they have finished reading a test. Talk about techniques for ensuring success, such as checking to make sure all answers are legible or revisiting more difficult questions. Ask student volunteers to explain what they do when they come across a difficult question. Do they leave it blank? Make a guess? Explain that there are techniques students can rely on to help them revisit these questions and answer them correctly.

Teaching Approach

Use of the Handbook
Read aloud or have a student volunteer read aloud the information under "Pause and Reflect" on pages 576–577 of the *Reader's Handbook*. Then walk students through the sample think-aloud on pages 577–578. Model the strategy by thinking aloud as you work through another one of the questions from the sample test. Discuss with students how the think aloud helped you answer the question. Then have students finish reading this section on their own.

Extend the Handbook
Have students work in pairs to practice visualizing and thinking aloud. Ask pairs to take turns thinking aloud as they revisit one of the test questions on pages 569–570. Work with partners to build an understanding of how this strategy can help them answer difficult questions.

Assessment
Ask students:

■ How can visualizing and thinking aloud help you reread difficult test questions?

■ What other After Reading techniques can you rely on during a test?

WEEK 32
Lesson 5 — Focus on Vocabulary Tests

For use with *Reader's Handbook* pages 584–587

Goals

In this lesson, students learn strategies for becoming successful vocabulary test-takers.

Teaching Focus

Background

Tips and techniques for building vocabulary are discussed in detail on pages 608–639 of the *Reader's Handbook*. Utilizing these techniques will significantly improve students' chances of performing well on vocabulary tests. But there are also specific tips students can rely on as they take vocabulary tests. This lesson concentrates on these tips.

Instruction

Ask students what they know about vocabulary tests. Discuss the types of questions students would expect to see on vocabulary tests. Explain that some content area tests, such as social studies or science tests, include sections on vocabulary. Talk about ways students prepare for these types of vocabulary tests. Point out that other times an entire test focuses on vocabulary. Explain that it is more difficult to "cram" for this type of test, but there are strategies that can improve students' performance on these tests as well.

Teaching Approach

Use of the Handbook

Have students work with a partner to preview this section of the *Reader's Handbook* (pages 584–587). Then have them read page 584 independently. Divide the class into four groups. Assign each group one of the four tips discussed in this section. Ask groups to explain their tip to the rest of the class. Then ask students to read page 587 on their own.

Extend the Handbook

Have students follow the tips on page 585 to create flash cards or a vocabulary notebook for a content area of their choice. Ask students to begin by listing key words from the chapter they are currently using in one of their textbooks. Remind them to review the words often.

Assessment

Ask students:

■ What are four techniques you can use to help you take vocabulary tests?

■ Which technique do you think will be the most difficult for you to use? What can you do to make it easier?

WEEK 32
Lesson 6 — Focus on Social Studies Tests

For use with *Reader's Handbook* pages 588–592

Goals

In this lesson, students examine techniques for taking social studies tests successfully.

Teaching Focus

Background

There are a variety of techniques that will help students prepare for and take social studies tests. Students will benefit from a detailed examination of these techniques, including ruling out obvious wrong answers and analyzing the questions for clues.

Instruction

Ask student volunteers to share what they do to get ready for a social studies test. List their study methods on the board. Then ask volunteers to share any strategies they use while taking social studies tests, such as crossing off obvious wrong answers or skimming the tests before starting. Explain that in this lesson students will explore these and other techniques for taking social studies tests.

Teaching Approach

Use of the Handbook

Have students read page 588 of the *Reader's Handbook* on their own. Then have three volunteers read aloud the tips on page 589. Discuss the purpose of each tip. Have volunteers continue reading aloud tips #5 through #8 (pages 590–591). Walk through the sample questions with students, pointing out how to use the tips as you go. Ask students to finish reading this section independently.

Extend the Handbook

Have students create tip sheets to keep in their social studies folders. Encourage them to list the tips discussed in this section of the handbook and then summarize how to use each tip in their own words. They might also include any additional activities students talked about in the beginning of the lesson.

For more practice, see pages 212–213 of the *Student Applications Book 6.*

Assessment

Ask students:

■ What techniques can you use to help you prepare for a social studies test?

■ What tips can you follow during the test to help you answer questions successfully?

WEEK 32
Lesson 7   Focus on Math Tests

For use with *Reader's Handbook* pages 593–597

Goals

In this lesson, students explore techniques for preparing for and taking math tests.

Teaching Focus

Background

Math tests are markedly different from other content area tests; they often require memorization of important formulas and quick computation. Successful math test-takers recognize that there are techniques they can use to help them prepare for and take math tests.

Instruction

Ask student volunteers to share what they do to prepare for a math test. Do they make use of practice tests at the end of a chapter? Review key terms? List their responses on the board. Work with students to compare the ways they study for math tests with how they study for other types of tests. Then have volunteers share techniques they use during math tests. Again, discuss the similarities and differences between math tests and other content area tests. Explain that while math tests are very different from social studies or science tests, there are general methods that work for all types of tests. Point out that in this lesson students will review these general techniques as well as learn ones specific to math tests.

Teaching Approach

Use of the Handbook

Have students read page 593 of the *Reader's Handbook* on their own. Review general techniques for preparing for tests, such as getting a good night's sleep and reviewing key terms. Then walk students through the four steps for finding the right answer on pages 594–596. Discuss the purpose for each step. Ask students to work in pairs to examine After Reading suggestions for solving math questions on pages 596–597.

Extend the Handbook

Have students practice the techniques learned in this section of the handbook by using pages 214–215 of the *Student Applications Book 6.*

Assessment

Ask students:

■ What techniques can you use to help you answer difficult questions on a math test?

■ Which technique do you think will be most helpful to you? Explain your choice.

WEEK 32
Lesson 8 Focus on Science Tests

For use with *Reader's Handbook* pages 598–605

Goals

In this lesson, students examine techniques for preparing for and taking science tests.

Teaching Focus

Background

As with other content area tests, successful test-takers recognize that there are techniques they can utilize to perform well on science tests. Exploring these activities, in particular techniques for reading graphics, will provide students with the tools necessary to work through science test questions effectively.

Instruction

Review with students what they have learned about test taking throughout this unit. What techniques do they find most helpful? Explain that in this last lesson, they will look at one more type of test—science tests. Discuss how science tests differ from other types of tests. What techniques do students predict they will learn about in this lesson?

Teaching Approach

Use of the Handbook

Have students work in small groups to preview the Focus on Science Tests section (pages 598–605) in the *Reader's Handbook*. Then come together as a class and walk through the section together. Ask student volunteers to read the four tips on page 599. Then think aloud as you work through the sample graphics on pages 600–604. (If students need additional background on reading graphics, see pages 538–561 of the handbook.) Finish this section by having students read page 605 independently. Return to the predictions students made at the beginning of the lesson, and compare them to the actual tips discussed in the section.

Extend the Handbook

To deepen students' understanding of the techniques they can use for science tests, have them complete pages 216–217 of the *Student Applications Book 6*.

Assessment

Ask students:

■ What techniques can you use to perform well on science tests?

■ What is the most important thing you learned about test-taking from this unit? Explain your answer.

WEEK 33

Improving Vocabulary

For use with *Reader's Handbook* pages 608–629

Daily Lessons	Summary*
Lesson 1 **Improving Vocabulary:** **An Overview**	Have students preview this section of the *Reader's Handbook*, and discuss ways of increasing their vocabulary.
Lesson 2 **Becoming a** **Word Collector**	Build an understanding of techniques students can use to learn new words. Have students create vocabulary journals or flash cards.
Lesson 3 **Making Words Your Own**	Work with students to explore techniques for moving new words from short-term to long-term memory.
Lesson 4 **Using a Dictionary**	Review with students parts of dictionary entries. Help students understand how to determine which definition to use for words with multiple meanings.

*Use these notes to help you teach a mini-lesson or to teach a briefer, shorter version of the lessons for more proficient students.

Lesson Resources

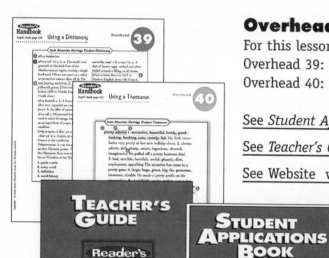

Overheads
For this lesson, use:
Overhead 39: Using a Dictionary
Overhead 40: Using a Thesaurus

See *Student Applications Book 6* pages 218–223.

See *Teacher's Guide* pages 415–428.

See Website www.greatsource.com/rehand/

For more practice, see also *Sourcebook* Grade 6, pages 68–74, 190–200; *Daybook* Grade 6, pages 26–31, 48–51.

WEEK 34

Improving Vocabulary (continued)

For use with *Reader's Handbook* pages 630–639

Daily Lessons	Summary*
Lesson 5 **Using a Thesaurus**	Work with students as they examine the parts of a thesaurus. Discuss how using a thesaurus can boost students' vocabulary.
Lesson 6 **Understanding Word Parts**	Build an understanding of how to use word parts to unlock the meaning of unfamiliar words.
Lesson 7 **Understanding Specialized Terms**	Help students learn techniques they can use to understand specialized terms. Have students look for examples of specialized terminology in a content area textbook.
Lesson 8 **Understanding Analogies**	Walk students through the steps involved in recognizing the relationships in basic analogies. Have students create their own analogies.

*Use these notes to help you teach a mini-lesson or to teach a briefer, shorter version of the lessons for more proficient students.

Lesson Resources

Overheads

For this lesson, use:
Overhead 39: Using a Dictionary
Overhead 40: Using a Thesaurus

See *Student Applications Book 6* pages 218–223.

See *Teacher's Guide* pages 414–428.

See Website www.greatsource.com/rehand/

For more practice, see also *Sourcebook* Grade 6, pages 68–74, 190–200; *Daybook* Grade 6, pages 26–31, 48–51.

WEEK 33
Lesson 1 Improving Vocabulary: An Overview

For use with *Reader's Handbook* pages 608–614, 621–623, 626–639

Goals

In this lesson, students preview this section of the *Reader's Handbook* and discuss methods of increasing their vocabulary.

Teaching Focus

Background

Vocabulary acquisition and reading comprehension are closely linked. Proficient readers not only have a large vocabulary of familiar words—they also have a repertoire of methods of learning new ones. This unit provides students with a variety of techniques to help build their vocabulary.

Instruction

To activate students' prior knowledge of vocabulary strategies, create a Concept Map for *vocabulary*. (See page 670 of the *Reader's Handbook* for more information on Concept Maps.) Ask students what they think of when they hear the word *vocabulary*. List their answers on the Concept Map. Explain that in this section of the handbook students will learn ways of boosting their vocabulary.

Teaching Approach

Use of the Handbook

Read aloud page 608 of the *Reader's Handbook*. Review previewing. Then have students preview the remainder of this section (pages 609–614, 621–623, 626–639) either in pairs or on their own. Remind students to pay attention to headings, graphics, and anything else that piques their curiosity about the material.

Extend the Handbook

Have students reflect on the preview by jotting down their thoughts about it in their journals. Questions for them to consider: What did I learn from the preview? What do I expect this section will be about? What do I hope to learn from reading it?

Assessment

Ask students:

■ What is the advantage of having a large vocabulary?

■ How would you rate your vocabulary now? Do you think this section will help you improve it? Why or why not?

WEEK 33
Lesson 2 Becoming a Word Collector

For use with *Reader's Handbook* pages 609–612

Goals

In this lesson, students explore techniques for learning new words.

Teaching Focus

Background

In order to construct meaning from a text, readers must first understand the words, or vocabulary, used in it. There are a variety of techniques available for comprehending unfamiliar words, including using context clues and breaking words into parts; the method used often depends on the word itself. This unit, with its focus on a variety of techniques for boosting vocabulary, serves as an excellent introduction to vocabulary acquisition.

Instruction

Discuss what students do when they come across an unfamiliar word. Do they skip the word and move on or try to figure out what the word means? Explain that when an unfamiliar word is important to the meaning of the sentence, skipping over it is not the best decision. Point out that there are techniques students can use to unlock the meaning of these words. Ask student volunteers to share methods that they use to figure out a word's meaning.

Teaching Approach

Use of the Handbook

Have students work in small groups to read through pages 609–612 of the *Reader's Handbook*. Have groups discuss the four steps for learning new words. Encourage students to share their thoughts about applying these steps to new words. Which steps have they tried before? Which steps are new to them?

Extend the Handbook

Have students begin a vocabulary journal or a set of vocabulary flash cards. Ask them to skim a chapter in a novel or textbook they are reading and write down five to ten unfamiliar words. Remind them to follow the steps in the *Reader's Handbook* for learning the words.

For more practice, see pages 218–219 of the *Student Applications Book 6*.

Assessment

Ask students:

■ What are the four steps for learning new words?

■ Do you think that following these steps will help you as you read? Why or why not?

WEEK 33
Lesson 3 Making Words Your Own

For use with *Reader's Handbook* pages 612–614

Goals

In this lesson, students examine methods for integrating new words into their personal vocabularies.

Teaching Focus

Background

Research studies have shown that it takes repeated exposure to move a new word from short-term to long-term memory. Students will benefit from an examination of techniques they can use to facilitate this process and make vocabulary words their own.

Instruction

Ask student volunteers to share their techniques for memorizing information, such as a friend's phone number or email address. Discuss how long it takes for them to memorize the information. Point out the difference between short-term and long-term memory. Explain that it often takes seven or eight exposures to new information before it becomes part of our long-term memory.

Teaching Approach

Use of the Handbook

Read aloud the top of page 612 of the *Reader's Handbook*. Then ask student volunteers to read aloud the steps under "Memorizing Words." Have students continue reading pages 612–614 of the handbook independently.

Extend the Handbook

Ask students to apply the steps discussed earlier to a few more unfamiliar words from their current reading material. Have students repeat the steps over the next week. Then ask them to reflect on how well the activity worked. Do they feel as though these words are now part of their personal word collection? If not, what more can they do to move the words into their long-term memory?

For more practice, see pages 218–219 of the *Student Applications Book 6*.

Assessment

Ask students:

■ How can you move words from short-term to long-term memory?

■ Why is it important to move words into long-term memory?

WEEK 33
Lesson 4 Using a Dictionary

For use with *Reader's Handbook* pages 626–629

Goals

In this lesson, students examine the parts of a dictionary and how dictionaries can help them boost their vocabulary.

Teaching Focus

Background

Dictionaries can be excellent tools for vocabulary acquisition if students know how to use them. Since so many English words have multiple meanings, students need instruction on how to determine which definition matches their inquiry. Students will also benefit from a review of the parts of dictionary entries. Students who have been using a dictionary for years are still often surprised by all the information a dictionary contains.

Instruction

Ask students to recall the parts of dictionary definitions, such as word histories, parts of speech, and pronunciations. Explain that since many words have more than one meaning, dictionary entries contain more than one definition. Discuss how students decide which definition to use. Explain that in this lesson students will learn more about the different parts of a dictionary entry and how to choose the correct definition.

Teaching Approach

Use of the Handbook

Have students read pages 626–627 of the *Reader's Handbook* on their own. Then discuss the differences among the three sample dictionary definitions. Do all three answer the four questions from page 627? What conclusions can students draw about the different dictionaries and their purposes? Walk students through the eight parts of dictionary definitions listed on page 629. Discuss the purpose of each part. Then review the information about how to determine the correct definition.

Extend the Handbook

Have students take turns picking a word with multiple meanings from the dictionary (such as *notice, practice,* or *example*). Have students use the word in a sentence, and then ask the rest of their group to find the correct definition in the dictionary.

For more practice, see page 209 of the *Student Applications Book 6*.

Assessment

Ask students:

■ What are three things you would expect to find in a dictionary entry?

■ How can you decide which definition to use when a word has more than one meaning?

WEEK 34
Lesson 5 ▸ Using a Thesaurus

For use with *Reader's Handbook* page 630

Goals

In this lesson, students examine a thesaurus and explore its use.

Teaching Focus

Background

Like dictionaries, thesauruses can be wonderful tools for boosting vocabulary. And, like a dictionary, a thesaurus is only as good as readers make it. An examination of the characteristics of a thesaurus and the benefits of using one will help students get the most out of this resource.

Instruction

Discuss students' prior knowledge of what a *thesaurus* is. Have they used one in the past? What do students think the purpose of a thesaurus is? Explain that writers rely on thesauruses to add variety to their word usage. Ask student volunteers to share words that they might overuse in their conversations or writing, such as *nice, happy*, or *pretty*. Brainstorm synonyms for *pretty*. Point out that in this lesson students will learn how to use a thesaurus to help them find replacements for overused words and boost their vocabulary in general.

Teaching Approach

Use of the Handbook

Walk students through the sample thesaurus entry on page 630 of the *Reader's Handbook*. Point out the various parts of the entry. Remind students that for words with multiple meanings, they must first determine which meaning most closely matches their inquiry. Compare the list of synonyms the class came up with for the word *pretty* with those listed in the sample thesaurus entry. Talk about the benefits of using thesauruses.

Extend the Handbook

Have students choose a brief sample of their writing, from either their writing portfolios or their journals. Ask them to use a thesaurus to find replacements for a few words from the text. Remind them to choose alternatives that do not change the basic meaning of the word. For example, students might replace a word that has a broad, general meaning with a more specific alternative. Encourage students to share both the original and rewritten pieces with a partner. How do they compare?

Assessment

Ask students:

■ How can using a thesaurus boost your vocabulary?

■ How would you explain to a friend what a thesaurus is?

210

WEEK 34
Lesson 6   Understanding Word Parts

For use with *Reader's Handbook* pages 621–625, 685–688

Goals

In this lesson, students learn how to use word parts to help them unlock the meaning of unfamiliar words.

Teaching Focus

Background

Proficient readers use familiar word parts to arrive at the meaning of unfamiliar words. Common prefixes, suffixes, and roots provide clues to word meanings. Developing students' knowledge of these common word parts will enhance their vocabulary and reading comprehension.

Instruction

Write the following words on the board: *enumerate, antiwar, bountiful*. Think aloud as you define each word by concentrating on its familiar parts (*numer, anti-, -ful*). Point out that readers often rely on word parts that they know to help them unlock the meaning of words they don't know. Review the terms *prefix, suffix*, and *root*. Explain that in this lesson students will learn how using word parts can boost their vocabulary.

Teaching Approach

Use of the Handbook

Read aloud the first few paragraphs on page 621 of the *Reader's Handbook*. Then have students read about prefixes, suffixes, and root words on pages 621–622. Work through the list of tips on page 623. Have students keep the tips in mind as they look over the list of prefixes, suffixes, and roots on pages 685–688 of the Almanac. Talk about techniques students can use to help them learn these word parts.

Extend the Handbook

Have students review their vocabulary journals or flash cards to find words whose meanings can be determined by breaking them into parts. As they review the words, remind students to refer to the list of common prefixes, suffixes, and roots on pages 685–688 of the Almanac.

Assessment

Ask students:

■ How can breaking a word into parts help you unlock its meaning?

■ Choose a prefix or suffix with which you are familiar. What does the prefix or suffix mean? List four words that include this word part.

WEEK 34
Lesson 7 — Understanding Specialized Terms

For use with *Reader's Handbook* pages 631–634

Goals

In this lesson, students build an understanding of techniques they can utilize to understand specialized terms.

Teaching Focus

Background

As students progress through school they will be exposed to more and more specialized terminology. Developing a repertoire of methods for understanding these terms now will benefit them through the remainder of their school career.

Instruction

Write the following on the board: *igobotck, limited viritiy, optolegumation*. Ask students what they would do if they came across these words in their science or math textbooks. How would they unlock the meaning of these words? Explain that while these examples are made up, they could just as well be part of a specialized language with which students are unfamiliar. Point out that years ago, if someone had mentioned *gigabyte, Internet,* and *cyberspace*, most people would have been stumped; today, these terms are familiar to most computer users. Explain that these are all examples of specialized language, terms that are used in specific circumstances and are often unfamiliar to the general population.

Teaching Approach

Use of the Handbook

Have students work in pairs to read pages 631–633 of the *Reader's Handbook*. Walk students through the tips for learning school terms on page 632. Then discuss how Concept Maps can help students understand and remember specialized terminology.

Extend the Handbook

Have students apply the techniques they learned for understanding specialized terms by previewing a new chapter in a content area textbook. Encourage them to follow the tips on page 632 and to create a Concept Map for one of the unfamiliar terms. Ask students to reflect on the activity. Did the tips or the Concept Map help them understand the terms?

Assessment

Ask students:

■ What is specialized terminology?

■ What techniques can you use to determine the meaning of specialized terms?

WEEK 34
Lesson 8 Understanding Analogies

For use with *Reader's Handbook* pages 636–639

Goals

In this lesson, students develop an understanding of basic analogies.

Teaching Focus

Background

Developing an understanding of analogies not only improves students' vocabulary, but also fosters their logical reasoning and flexible thinking skills. Analogies can be intimidating for students at first. The basic overview presented in this lesson will build students' confidence in their ability to read and understand these relationships.

Instruction

Write the following on the board: *king : queen :: husband : wife*. Assess students' prior knowledge of analogies by asking volunteers to explain what this means. Lead students to see that it is an example of an analogy. Explain that analogies show similarities between two things. Point out that this analogy can be read as *"King* is to *queen* as *husband* is to *wife."* Compare the relationship between kings and queens and husbands and wives. Do students recognize that a king and a queen are specific examples of a husband and wife relationship?

Teaching Approach

Use of the Handbook

Since analogies may be difficult for students to grasp at first, divide the class into small groups and move from group to group to provide instruction. Have students read the bottom of page 636 of the *Reader's Handbook*. Then think aloud as you work through the sample analogy at the bottom of the page. Walk students through the various types of analogies on pages 637–639. Depending on your assessment of students' understanding of analogies, either continue to think aloud as you work through the analogies or guide students as they move toward identifying the relationships independently.

Extend the Handbook

Challenge students to create their own analogies using some of the categories listed on pages 637–639. Encourage students to share their analogies with the class.

Assessment

Ask students:

■ What is an analogy?

■ How will you use the information in this section to boost your vocabulary?

WEEK 35

Strategy Handbook

For use with *Reader's Handbook* pages 644–647, 650–651, 658–659

Daily Lessons	Summary*
Lesson 1 **Looking for Cause and Effect**	Help students understand strategies for identifying cause-effect relationships. Have students create Cause-Effect Organizers for a newspaper or magazine article.
Lesson 2 **Effective Note-taking**	Build an understanding of note-taking strategies. Have students use one of the techniques from the lesson to take notes on a chapter in a textbook.
Lesson 3 **Paraphrasing**	Work with students to explore how to use the reading strategy of paraphrasing. Have students paraphrase part of a chapter from a textbook.
Lesson 4 **Summarizing**	Walk students through techniques for summarizing effectively. Compare the strategies of summarizing and paraphrasing.

*Use these notes to help you teach a mini-lesson or to teach a briefer, shorter version of the lessons for more proficient students.

Lesson Resources

See *Teacher's Guide* pages 429–441.

See Website www.greatsource.com/rehand/

Reading Tools

For use with *Reader's Handbook* pages 666–684

Daily Lessons	**Summary***
Lesson 1 **Reading Tools: Fiction**	Review with students how and why to use organizers when reading fiction. Discuss the purposes of various organizers.
Lesson 2 **Reading Tools: Nonfiction**	Help students explore the organizers available for understanding nonfiction material.
Lesson 3 **Reading Tools: Persuasive Writing**	Reinforce the importance of using organizers to help students understand and evaluate persuasive writing. Have students use a reading tool as they read an editorial.
Lesson 4 **The *Reader's Handbook*: A Review**	Discuss what students have learned from using the *Reader's Handbook*. Have them reflect on their experiences in their journals.

*Use these notes to help you teach a mini-lesson or to teach a briefer, shorter version of the lessons for more proficient students.

Lesson Resources

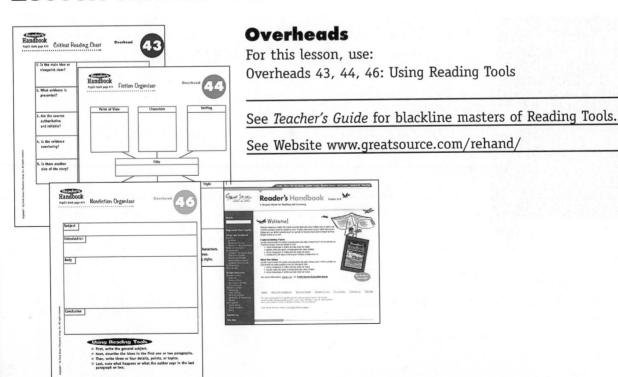

Overheads

For this lesson, use:

Overheads 43, 44, 46: Using Reading Tools

See *Teacher's Guide* for blackline masters of Reading Tools.

See Website www.greatsource.com/rehand/

WEEK 35
Lesson 1 ▶ Looking for Cause and Effect

For use with *Reader's Handbook* pages 644–645

Goals

In this lesson, students explore the strategy for identifying cause-effect relationships in both fiction and nonfiction.

Teaching Focus

Background

Throughout the *Reader's Handbook* students have explored strategies for understanding a variety of texts, from short stories to textbooks. The Strategy Handbook section of the *Reader's Handbook* focuses on 12 of the strategies students can use to become more proficient readers. Most of these have already been introduced earlier in the handbook; for some students this will serve as a review and a reminder of the importance of using these strategies. In this lesson, students will review how to identify cause-effect relationships.

Instruction

Discuss how students would define a reading strategy. Lead students to see that reading strategies are approaches for understanding and finding meaning in what they read. Explain that in this unit they will look at four essential reading strategies in detail. This first lesson concentrates on looking for cause and effect.

Teaching Approach

Use of the Handbook

Review the terms *cause* and *effect* with students. Remind them that a cause is something that happens first; effects are the results of the initial action. Then walk students though the information on cause and effect on pages 644–645 of the *Reader's Handbook*. Discuss how identifying cause-effect relationships can help students understand what they read. Review the tools on these pages. Explain that Cause-Effect Organizers can help students see the relationship between the causes and effects.

Extend the Handbook

Have students look through the local newspaper for examples of cause-effect relationships. Ask them to create a Cause-Effect Organizer to show the relationship.

Assessment

Ask students:

■ What is a cause-effect relationship?

■ Why is it important to identify cause-effect relationships when reading?

WEEK 35
Lesson 2 — Effective Note-taking

For use with *Reader's Handbook* pages 646–647

Goals

In this lesson, students learn strategies for taking notes effectively.

Teaching Focus

Background

Effective notes enable students to organize, highlight, and review important information from a text. The key to effective note-taking is determining what information warrants inclusion. A general review of main ideas and details will refresh students' memories of strategies for identifying important information. This lesson focuses on four techniques for organizing notes.

Instruction

Discuss the benefits of taking notes. Point out that good notes should be all students need to review and remember the important information from a text. Talk about what students do when they are asked to take notes. How do they decide what information to include in their notes? How do they organize their notes? Explain that there are a variety of notes. Deciding what type to use depends on the text involved.

Teaching Approach

Use of the Handbook

Walk students through the four types of note-taking tools on pages 646–647 of the *Reader's Handbook*. (For more information on Class and Text Notes, see page 669 of the handbook.) Point out the differences among the types as you read. Build an understanding of the purposes of each type. Model effective note-taking by thinking aloud as you read a paragraph or two from a chapter in a content area textbook. Point out the information that you would include in your notes and which note-taking technique you would use.

Extend the Handbook

Have students use one of the four tools to take notes on a chapter from a class novel or textbook. Remind students to concentrate on main events and ideas as they work.

Assessment

Ask students:

■ What are the benefits of taking notes?

■ Which note-taking tool would you use if you were reading about the history of space travel? Explain your choice.

WEEK 35
Lesson 3 Paraphrasing

For use with *Reader's Handbook* pages 650–651

Goals

In this lesson, students explore how to use the reading strategy of paraphrasing.

Teaching Focus

Background

Paraphrasing can be a powerful strategy for constructing meaning from texts. By putting information in our own words, we automatically become more invested in the material. Paraphrasing enables readers to make sense out of difficult texts and to deepen understanding of more accessible ones.

Instruction

Ask students what it means to "use your own words." Discuss situations in which they are expected to use their own words. Point out that when they put something in their own words, they are paraphrasing. Discuss the importance of paraphrasing when students research information for their own writing. Point out that they shouldn't use many quotes in their paraphrases but that when they do quote, they need to use quotation marks to show that text has been picked up word for word.

Teaching Approach

Use of the Handbook

Read aloud or have a student volunteer read aloud the first two paragraphs on page 650 of the *Reader's Handbook*. Then walk students through the steps for using the strategy on pages 650 and 651. Model the strategy for students by reading an excerpt from a novel or informational book and paraphrasing the material.

Extend the Handbook

Ask students to apply the steps for paraphrasing to a current chapter in a content area textbook. Remind students to preview, take notes, and put the material in their own words. After students complete the activity, ask them to reflect on it in their journals. Questions to consider: How difficult was it for me to paraphrase this information? How did paraphrasing affect my understanding of the material?

Assessment

Ask students:

■ What steps do you follow to paraphrase material?

■ Why is it important to paraphrase what you read?

218

WEEK 35
Lesson 4 ▶ Summarizing

For use with *Reader's Handbook* pages 658–659

Goals

In this lesson, students examine techniques for summarizing effectively.

Teaching Focus

Background

Proficient readers summarize all types of reading material. As with other reading strategies, summarizing enables readers to take an active role in the reading process. Summarizing fosters deeper understanding of the text and is an excellent strategy for remembering main ideas and important details.

Instruction

Discuss with students what they think it means to summarize. Lead students to see that summarizing means to retell just the key events or ideas in their own words. Discuss the differences between summarizing and paraphrasing. Help students understand that while both require readers to retell information in their own words, summaries include only main ideas. Therefore, summaries are often shorter and more to the point than paraphrases.

Teaching Approach

Use of the Handbook

Read aloud or have a student volunteer read aloud the top of page 658 of the *Reader's Handbook*. Then walk students through the techniques for using the strategy on pages 658–659. Compare summarizing fiction and nonfiction material, and work through the two tools in this section. Talk about how these organizers can help students summarize information. Lead students to recognize that summarizing information in their own words will help them recognize key information and remember what they read.

Extend the Handbook

Have students choose an article from a newspaper or magazine to summarize for the class. Remind them to use the techniques for summarizing nonfiction on page 659 of the handbook. Encourage them to create a Nonfiction Organizer, such as the one on page 659, to help them organize their summary.

Assessment

Ask students:

■ What is the purpose of summarizing?

■ What would you look for when you summarize fiction? What would you look for when you summarize nonfiction?

WEEK 36
Lesson 1
Reading Tools: Fiction

For use with *Reader's Handbook* pages 666, 671, 677, 679

Goals

In this lesson, students review how and why to use reading tools when reading fiction.

Teaching Focus

Background

Students were introduced to the use of tools with fiction earlier in the *Reader's Handbook*. This lesson introduces three additional tools that students can use to deepen their understanding of the story's point of view, setting, characters, plot, and theme.

Instruction

Review with students the five main story elements (point of view, setting, characters, plot, and theme) and the corresponding tools introduced earlier in the handbook (that is, Character Development Chart, Character Map, Plot Diagram, Storyboard). Ask student volunteers to explain how they use reading tools to help them read short stories, plays, and novels. Explain that there are additional tools available for understanding fiction.

Teaching Approach

Use of the Handbook

Explore the unit opener for the Reading Tools section of the *Reader's Handbook* on page 666. Explain that this section includes examples of all the tools discussed in the handbook. Point out that the reading tools are listed here in alphabetical order. Walk through the list with students. Ask them to make note of the organizers that they use currently. Encourage them to add additional organizers to their "tool kit." Then work with students to explore three additional useful tools for fiction: Fiction Organizer (page 671), Setting Chart (page 677), and Story String (page 679). Discuss the purposes of each. Talk about how students can decide which tool to use when they are reading fiction.

Extend the Handbook

Ask students to use one of the tools introduced in this lesson for a piece of fiction they are currently reading. Have student volunteers share with the class what they learned from creating the tools.

Assessment

Ask students:

■ What is the purpose of a Fiction Organizer? A Setting Chart? A Story String?

■ How would you decide which of these reading tools to use?

WEEK 36
Lesson 2 Reading Tools: Nonfiction

For use with *Reader's Handbook* pages 673, 675, and 677

Goals

In this lesson, students examine the various reading tools available for understanding nonfiction material.

Teaching Focus

Background

A variety of graphic organizers were introduced in the sections Reading Textbooks and Reading Nonfiction. Here, students review these organizers and their purposes. Students are also introduced to three additional graphic organizers they can use with nonfiction material.

Instruction

Review with students tools they can use to help them understand nonfiction material, such as Cause-Effect Organizers, 5 W's Organizers, and Timelines. Talk about students' experiences with organizers and nonfiction. What organizers do students rely on when they read nonfiction? How do the tools help them? Explain that in this lesson students will examine three more tools to use with nonfiction material: K-W-L Chart, Nonfiction Organizer, and Process Notes.

Teaching Approach

Use of the Handbook

Work with students as they examine the three new tools. Begin with the K-W-L Chart on page 673 of the *Reader's Handbook*. (K-W-L Charts are quite common; students might be familiar with them already. Even so, they most likely have not been taught to use them independently.) Discuss how a K-W-L Chart can help them set a purpose for reading. Next, walk through the Nonfiction Organizer on page 675. Talk about how this organizer can help them break down the information in a text. Finally, explore the Process Notes on page 677. Discuss the differences between Process Notes and a Timeline.

Extend the Handbook

Have students create a Nonfiction Organizer for a newspaper or magazine article. Talk about how the tool affected their understanding of the material.

Assessment

Ask students:

■ What is the purpose of a K-W-L Chart? A Nonfiction Organizer? Process Notes?

■ How will you decide which reading tool to use when you read nonfiction?

WEEK 36
Lesson 3 Reading Tools: Persuasive Writing

For use with *Reader's Handbook* pages 667, 670, and 683

Goals

In this lesson, students review reading tools they can use to understand and evaluate persuasive writing.

Teaching Focus

Background

The purpose of persuasive writing is to express an opinion and convince others to share it. One purpose when reading persuasive writing is to understand and evaluate the opinion and decide whether you (the reader) agree with it or not. The Reading Tools section of the Reader's Almanac includes several tools designed to help readers evaluate persuasive writing.

Instruction

Review what students know about persuasive writing. Remind students that persuasive writing is used to express an opinion, and talk about the importance of evaluating persuasive writing. Remind students that there are reading tools available to help them evaluate persuasive writing.

Teaching Approach

Use of the Handbook

Review three tools that might be especially useful for evaluating persuasive writing introduced: Argument Chart (page 667), Critical Reading Chart (page 670), and Viewpoint and Evidence Organizer (page 683). Walk students through each tool. Discuss the similarities and differences among the three. You might create a Venn Diagram to illustrate these similarities and differences. Use the comparisons to help students understand the purposes of each.

Extend the Handbook

Ask students to create an Argument Chart, Critical Reading Chart, and Viewpoint and Evidence Organizer for an editorial or other piece of persuasive writing. Have students work in small groups to discuss how each organizer helped them evaluate the material.

Assessment

Ask students:

■ How can reading tools help you evaluate persuasive writing?

■ Which of the three tools discussed in this lesson do you think will help you evaluate persuasive writing most effectively? Explain your choice.

WEEK 36
Lesson 4
The *Reader's Handbook*: A Review

For use with the *Reader's Handbook* as a whole

Goals

In this lesson, students reflect on what they learned from the *Reader's Handbook* and how they can use it in the future to help them get the most out of their reading.

Teaching Focus

Background

After working through the *Reader's Handbook*, it is important to bring closure to the process by reviewing key components and reflecting on what students have learned throughout the year. Reviewing and reflecting on their work with the handbook will reinforce students' understanding and promote their continued use of the strategies and tools taught throughout the handbook.

Instruction

Discuss with students what they learned from using the *Reader's Handbook*. Ask them to think back to the beginning of the handbook. How has their understanding of the reading process changed since then? Explain that students can use the strategies and tools introduced in the *Reader's Handbook* throughout the rest of their school career and beyond. Point out strategies and tools that you still use as you read.

Teaching Approach

Use of the Handbook

Review with students the Table of Contents on pages 4–12 of the *Reader's Handbook*. Discuss the various sections of the handbook. Talk about which section students found most helpful and which they found most difficult. Allow students time to review the section they found most difficult. Encourage them to list questions they have about the section and then skim the section for answers.

Extend the Handbook

Have students reflect on their use of the *Reader's Handbook* by jotting down their thoughts in their journals. Questions to consider: How has my use of the *Reader's Handbook* improved my reading ability? Am I a stronger reader now than I was before using the handbook? Why or why not?

Assessment

Ask students:

■ What has the *Reader's Handbook* taught you about reading?

■ Has your reading process changed? Explain.

Lessons Index